BURGESS
CAMPING
SERIES

CREATIVE NATURE CRAFTS

by

R. O. BALE

Commissioner
Schuyler County
Department of Social Services
Watkins Glen, New York

BURGESS PUBLISHING COMPANY
Minneapolis

PREFACE

Material for this edition of "CREATIVE NATURE CRAFTS" has been developing over a long period of years of teaching of both nature study and craft projects in a variety of camping and youth organizations in the northeastern part of the United States.

This material will be found useful in camping situations, and in other situations where crafts or nature study are a part of the program. It may be used by a teacher or instructor in planning and carrying on the program or it may be used by individuals of 8 to 80 in developing their own hobbies.

There were two primary purposes in the development of this book; the first being the development of craft projects using inexpensive materials readily available in nature; and the second being the use of interesting and creative crafts in teaching an understanding and appreciation of the beauties of nature.

The author of this publication has had some thirty years of experience in camping programs as a Director, Ass't. Director, Craft Instructor, Instructor in Camping and Woodcraft, Waterfront Director, Supervisor of Counsellor Training, and Guidance Counsellor; and has been active as an officer of the Upstate New York Section of the American Camping Association.

A great many persons have contributed ideas and suggestions which have been incorporated in this publication, and have assisted with the preparation of demonstrational materials and the conducting of workshops and leader-training programs. Others have helped with illustrations for this book.

TABLE OF CONTENTS

FOREWORD

By the use of materials from nature in craft projects we are
able to develop the ability to see many of the beautiful things
around us that we are otherwise apt to pass by without recog-
nition or understanding. Through them we also develop in-
genuity and imagination in the use and enjoyment of materials
found in nature. We learn to see and appreciate the subtle
colors, unusual shapes, and the wide varieties of texture
found in seeds, seed-pods, cones, twigs, leaves, flowers,
berries, fungi, moss, and lichens.

Such things as rocks, minerals, pieces of horn and antler,
bones, animal tracks, feathers, horsehair, porcupine quills,
bark, insects, and wildlife, each may have a place in nature
craft projects.

Most of these things may be found in relatively large quanti-
ties in nearby gardens, fields, woods, streams, and swamps.
Gathering, identifying, and storing them is an enjoyable activity in itself, and this collecting can be a year-round hobby
for the collected materials may be stored ready for the min-
ute when they are needed in a craft project. Storage, of
course, can be a problem - but boxes of assorted sizes will
help to solve it. Small boxes, bottles, and plastic containers
are excellent for storage. A dry place is essential for storing most of the collected items for mildew will soon spoil
native craft materials if they are stored where it is damp.
It is essential, too, that the materials themselves be well
dried before storing.

The best way to develop nature craft projects (and to enjoy
them), is to give the imagination free reign, and to experiment with the materials available.

If you are planning to teach crafts using native materials,
try to develop teaching materials that will stimulate creative
ideas, rather than making things that are to be copied. It is
almost impossible to be a "copy-cat" however, for there are
so many variations in materials, situations, and individuals.

The crafts described in this book will give some help on where
and how to get started, but they are by no means all of the

possibilities. We have made everything in this book, and in the process have come up with hundreds of variations and new ideas. You will find other possibilities, too, without a doubt. Materials are inexpensive and easy to find wherever you may live, although they may vary greatly from one part of the country to another. Many of the supplies needed will all ready be on hand. Others require a bit of hunting. Some will need to be purchased from the nearest store, a Craft Supply or Hobby Shop.

The following lists may be found useful, and can certainly be added to from the native materials found in any part of the country.

NATIVE MATERIALS

Acorns	Magnolia leaves
Bayberries	Milkweed pods and seeds
Birch bark and other barks	Moss
Bittersweet berries	Nuts
Bones	Pearly Everlasting flowers
Burdock burrs	Pits of apricot and peach
Cat-tails	Poppy seed-pods
Catalpa seed-pods	Reeds and rushes
Cones of all kinds	Rocks and minerals
Corn husks	Rose haws
Dried weed seed-pods	Straw
Drift wood	Strawflowers
Ferns	Sunflower seeds
Grains	Tag Alder seed-pods
Grasses	Teasel
Horn and antler	Trumpet vine seed-pods
Jersey tea	Tulip seed-pods
Leaves	Walnut shells
Lichens	Watermelon seeds
Lilac seed-pods	Witch-hazel seed-pods
Lily seed-pods	Witch-hazel wood

OTHER SUPPLIES

Cotton

Kitchen shears

Pliers and wire cutters

Toothpicks

Tweezers

SUPPLIES THAT MAY BE PURCHASED

Beads (Seed, wood, bamboo, pottery)

Christmas decorations (Small bells, balls, etc.)

Cork (Small pieces, or sheets 1/16 or 1/8 inch thick)

Earring backs or findings

Florist's tape (Green and brown)

Florist's wire

Household or model plane cement

Jump rings (Small metal)

Lacquer in spray cans (Clear, gold, silver, copper, etc.)

Pin backs (Metal or plastic)

Pipe cleaners

Plaster of Paris

Plastic rings and chains

Ribbon

Screw eyes (Tiny)

Sequins and glitter

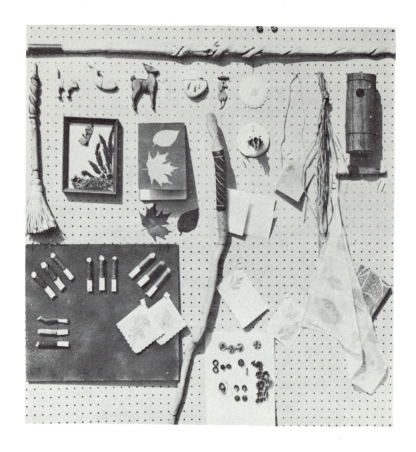

Display of NATURE CRAFTS including carved walking canes; wood carvings; witch-hazel broom; plaque; leaf prints made as spatter prints, smoke prints, and block prints; plaster casts; basswood bark cordage; basswood bark birdhouse; whistle; wood specimens; and native costume jewelry.

NATURE PRINTS

Prints of leaves, flowers, grasses and other plant materials, can be made by several methods. Each kind of print has its own peculiar charm and can be used in a variety of ways. The methods for making eleven types of prints listed here, are described in this book.

Blue Prints

Ozalid or Dry Prints

Smoke Prints

Ink Pad Prints

Crayon Prints

Spatter or Spray Prints

Block Prints

Printing With a Wooden Block

Rub Printing

Plaster Casting a Leaf

Dye Printing

The choice of the kind of print to be made depends upon:

1. The plant materials and the printing supplies available

2. The age, interest, and ability of the group

3. The amount of time available, and the time of day (A bright sun is needed for Blue Prints and Ozalid Prints)

4. The use to be made of the finished print

The materials that are needed for making each of these prints are inexpensive and generally available. Supplies may have to be ordered from craft supply houses if local stores do not carry all of the items needed.

The uses to which nature prints may be put depend upon the interests and the imagination of the individuals or the group. Generally speaking there are three uses with which this book is concerned.

1. To assist in learning to identify plant materials and to learn more about plants.

2. In making a record of a collection of leaves or other plant materials

3. To use as decorations (for gifts, on clothing, notebook covers, notepaper, Christmas cards, gift wrapping paper, place-mats, napkins, desk sets, pictures, scarves, neckties, skirts, aprons, etc.)

Spatter Prints and Crayon Prints are the easiest and least expensive to make. They may have limited use but are fun for small children. They show less detail than the other types of prints and so are not as useful for notebook collections or to be used for identification.

Blue Prints, Ozalid Prints, and Smoke Prints, can be used for identification, for making attractive notepaper, and for covering boxes and tin cans for a variety of uses. The decorative possibilities of these prints are unlimited. Some suggestions for their use are included in the directions for making the prints.

Block Prints, Spray, and Spatter Prints may be made directly on fabric if suitable inks or paints are used. If fabric is used, care must be taken in its selection. Heavy materials, and materials with a coarse weave do not take the prints satisfactorily.

BLUE PRINTS

Prints made on blue print paper will show the print in white on a deep blue background. Leaves, plants, and flowers with interesting outlines are best for this type of print as only the outline shows. Stems, blossoms, and leaves of a plant may be used together either as a record or in making a design; or a variety of plant materials of different shapes and sizes may be used in making a decorative print.

USES:

Notebook collections, or collections on single record cards - prints of single leaves or of complete plants may be used in making up a notebook showing varieties for identification or for a collection; or single prints may be put on file cards to be used for reference or for teaching purposes.

Large or small Blue Prints may be framed as wall decorations, or may be used on covers of notebooks or folders.

Covering small boxes or small tin cans for use on a desk or dresser as containers for such things as pencils, paper clips, bobby-pins, etc. The design of the print should be planned to fit the space to be covered, using a paper pattern cut to the correct size. Attach the print to box or tin can with library paste, mucilage or rubber cement.

MATERIALS:

Blue Print paper of medium speed for printing by exposure
to sunlight. Craft supply houses and architect's supply
centers are good sources of supply. Purchase the paper
cut to the desired size, or by the yard to be cut as needed.
Convenient sizes are 4 X 5 inches or 8-1/2 X 11 inches.

Keep the Blue Print paper wrapped and in a dark, dry
place. Use within a few weeks of purchasing. The paper
may be removed from the wrapping and cut to size in any
weak light, and the cut pieces kept in an envelope or box
until used. When cutting or handling be sure to keep the
paper away from any bright light until ready to expose
it to the sunlight.

1 piece of glass slightly larger than the Blue Print paper to
be used.

1 piece of heavy cardboard, wood, book, or magazine approximately the same size as the glass.

Small tweezers for handling plant materials

Masking tape

Pan of cold water

HOW TO MAKE:

Cover the edges of all glasses with masking tape - both for
safety and to provide a border for the finished print.
The masking tape will print its outline on the finished
print just the same as will the plant materials used.

Arrange the leaves, grass, or others materials to form a
desirable design on the glass.

Place a piece of blue-print paper over this arrangement, blue
side down. Cover the blue-print paper with a board or
book to hold the paper and the arrangement in place.

Take hold of both board and glass, turning the glass side up,
holding firmly so that the plant materials cannot slip.

Keep the fingers on the masking tape at the edge of the glass
so they will not show in the final print.

Expose the material to strong sunlight until the blueprint
paper fades to a greenish-gray color.

After exposure take the material to shade or better yet inside.
Remove the blue-print paper and immediately place the

4

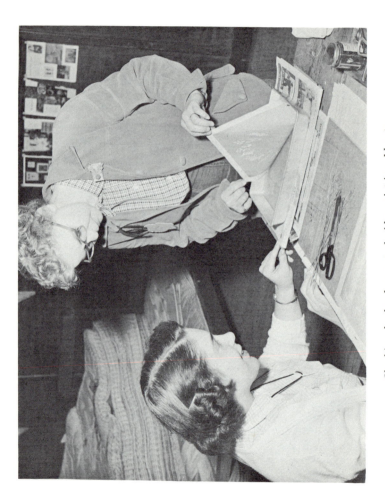

Checking the development of a blue print in cold water.
The arrangement of grasses is seen near the scissors.

exposed paper face down in a shallow pan of cold water.

Keep the paper covered with water for about five minutes or
until the color changes to a deep blue background with
the design in a clear white. A few drops of hydrogen
peroxide added to the water will give a very deep blue,
but is not necessary unless desired.

Remove the print from the water and dry on a flat surface.
To prevent wrinkling, the paper may be placed between
absorbent paper such as paper towels or blotters and
dried beneath a weight.

To attach blue prints or other paper decorations to tin cans
or boxes, an excellent paste may be made with flour and
hot water. To make the paste -

Mix 1 tablespoon flour with 1/4 cup of water (to mix
thoroughly shake in a tightly closed jar)

Pour into a small saucepan and cook until the mixture is thick and clear. Stir constantly. If the
paste is too thick, add a little more water. Stir
and let cool.

This paste will not stain and is inexpensive and easy to use.
Don't make a large quantity as it spoils quickly. A little
borax (1/4 teaspoon) added will help prevent spoilage.

OZALID OR DRY PRINTS

Prints made on ozalid or dry print paper are just the opposite
of blue prints in color. In other words, the design prints in
color while the background remains white. These prints
show detail very well and so can be used with delicate materials. Ozalid papers are available from supply houses in
a variety of colors.

USES:

Ozalid or dry prints can be used in the same manner as blue
prints, and in addition can be used to make beautiful
notepaper. Small leaf or flower prints are most effective in a corner of a sheet to be used as notepaper or as
a greeting card or place card. A border may be added
by use of a narrow mask covering from 1/8 to 1/4 inch
of the edge of the paper at the time the print is made.

OZALID PAPERS COME IN VARIOUS COLORS.
THEY ARE EXCELLENT FOR LEAF PRINTS,
AND MAKE VERY NICE NOTE PAPER.

MATERIALS:

Ozalid or dry print paper
    Buy it cut to the desired size or by the yard

Keep it wrapped in a dark dry place and use within a few
    weeks of purchasing. Open the package when needed,
    in a darkened place, handling in the same manner as
    the blue print paper.

1 piece of glass slightly larger than the ozalid paper to be
    used

1 piece of heavy cardboard, plywood, or book the same size
    as the glass.

Small tweezers for handling the plant materials.

Masking tape

Large glass jar with a tight cover (the jar should be large
enough to hold the exposed paper without wrinkling. The
paper may be rolled up but should not be folded. A large
mayonnaise or pickle jar is excellent).

Household ammonia

Small jar to hold ammonia (to be placed inside larger jar)

HOW TO MAKE:

Cover the edges of the glass with masking tape for safety;
to form a border for the finished print; and to afford a
place for the fingers to hold the material during exposure.

Have the large glass container ready with the small container
of ammonia inside, and a tight cover for the large jar.
A paper towel or facial tissue soaked with ammonia may
be substituted for the small container.

Arrange plant materials in a desired design on the glass.

Place the ozalid paper, glossy or yellow side down over the
arrangement, being careful not to expose the paper to a
any strong light while handling.

Place the board or book on the top of the arrangement to hold
the materials in place.

Take hold of the board and glass, turning the glass side up,
holding firmly so that the plant materials and paper
cannot slip.

Expose to strong sunlight until the paper turns white.

Remove materials from the bright sunlight and place the
exposed paper in the jar with the ammonia and close the
cover.

Watch the print develop in the ammonia fumes. Remove the
paper and turn it over and replace it in the jar if development is uneven.

Remove the print from the jar when the design has developed
to a deep even color.

SMOKE PRINTS

Smoke prints are delicate and detailed. They are easy for young children to make but any age group will find them fascinating. They are most effective on smooth, slightly absorbent paper such as mimeograph paper, in light colors.

Smoke prints are gray in color, but finely powdered colors may be dusted over them immediately after they are made, giving the effect of fall colors to leaf prints.

USES:

As a record of leaves collected in a nature study or forestry project.

As decorations on stationery, place cards, Christmas cards, or gift wrapping paper.

For wall decoration as a framed print.

MATERIALS:

Pieces of newspaper about 8 X 10 inches

Shortening or an unsalted butter

Candle stub or kerosene lamp

Mimeograph or other unglazed paper

Pan of water - for safety

Powdered tempera paints or metallic powders such as used in stenciling on furniture, if the print is to be colored.

HOW TO MAKE:

Prepare a sheet of smoked paper in the following manner:

Work on a pad of newspapers. Rub a small amount, less than 1/4 teaspoon, of shortening into a sheet of unglazed paper, being careful not to wrinkle the paper. Rub in well until the paper is translucent and no visible grease remains on the surface. This greased area need be but little larger than the size of the largest leaf to be printed, and need not cover the entire sheet of paper.

Turning the greased side of the paper down, pass it horizontally through the tip of the flame of a candle or lamp, keeping the paper in constant motion until the greased area is coated with a uniform velvety coating of smoke. Use care to prevent the paper touching the wick and leaving an oily spot on the paper. Keep the paper in constant motion, too, to prevent its scorching or catching fire. If it should catch fire, dunk it quickly in the pan of water kept on hand for that purpose, and start the process again with a fresh sheet of paper.

Prepare the leaf selected for printing by placing it on the smoked paper with the veined side of the leaf next to the smoked area. Cover the leaf with a piece of newspaper and rub over the leaf with the fingers of one hand while holding the paper and leaf in place with the other. The veins and edges of the leaf will quickly become well coated with the smoke.

Make the print by placing the leaf with the smoked side down on the material to be printed. Cover with a clean piece of newspaper, and rub carefully with the fingers of one hand while holding the leaf in place with the other. Rub from the center rib of the leaf outward. Moving the leaf while rubbing will cause a "double exposure" and spoil the print.

Remove the leaf and see the print.

With normal care this smoke print will not smudge. The same leaf may be used for several prints.

The print may be colored by dusting powdered tempera colors or metallic stencil powders over the print, or by tapping color on the print with the finger tip or a piece of facial tissue. Shake, blow, or brush excess color from the print. Spray with a fixative if the color tends to smudge.

INK PAD PRINTS

Prints of small leaves, grasses, and ferns may be made on paper, using "rubber stamp" ink pads which are available in in a variety of colors. This is a very handy method of making prints while on a hike or field trip, rather than collecting leaves which soon wilt.

10

USES:

A collection device for a notebook, or for future identification.

As a decoration for notepaper or cards.

MATERIALS:

Ink pad

Paper or notebook

Pieces of newspaper or other scrap paper about the size of
the ink pad.

HOW TO MAKE:

Place the leaf on the ink pad, veined side down.

Place a piece of scrap paper over the leaf and rub firmly with
the finger tips.

Remove the leaf from the ink pad and place it, inked side
down, on the paper to be printed. Cover with another
piece of paper and rub gently but firmly. Be careful
not to move the leaf and smudge the print.

Let dry before handling; or place between pieces of absorbent
paper.

CRAYON PRINTS

Sturdy leaves with strong veining and deeply cut margins are
best for this type of print. This is quickly and easily done
by small children and is similar to the way in which children
make "play money".

USES:

Decorative designs on paper or fabric

Cut-out decorations for wall or window

Notepaper or gift wrapping paper

Notebook or record book.

MATERIALS:

Crayons

Smooth paper

Scissors and paste

HOW TO MAKE:

Place paper over the leaf with the veined side up. Rub a
crayon gently but firmly over the leaf area with the
crayon strokes in one direction only. The area around
the leaf print may be decorated with crayons, or the
print may be cut out and pasted on the surface to be
decorated, or in a notebook.

SPATTER OR SPRAY PRINTS

Leaves, plants, and flowers with interesting outlines show
up well in this type of printing, but only the outline of the
plant material or leaf will show in the finished print. Spatter
prints may be made on either paper or fabric if suitable paints
are used.

USES:

Notebooks or record books

Place-mats of paper, fabric, or cork

Note paper

Gift wrapping paper

Christmas cards

Covers for books and folders

Pictures for wall decorations

Scarves and neckties

Pencil holders, paper-clip holders, etc. made with tin cans
and boxes

MATERIALS:

Poster paints; fabric paints that are fast to washing, or water
colors

Old tooth brushes

12

Window screening fastened over a small box, such as a cigar box with the bottom removed, or a small household sieve.

Small containers for mixing paints

Paper; smooth textured fabric; or sheet cork cut into sizes for place mats, coasters. etc.

Pins

Newspapers

(Spray paints or enamels in pressure cans, or in small hand sprayers, may be used in place of the tooth brushes and screening, or sieve.)

Spatter prints are often used for leaf collections
or for decoration of programs, notebooks, etc.

HOW TO MAKE:

Press the plant material to be used until it will lay flat.

Place the paper, cloth, or cork to be decorated, on a flat surface.

Protect the surrounding area with newspapers.

Arrange the plant materials in a desired design on the material to be printed and fasten in place with pins.

Dip the tooth brush in the paint; shake off the excess paint and run the brush over the screen or sieve held at least two inches from the materials being printed. A little experimentation will show the proper height for the best effect. Move the screening around so that a fine spatter of paint is produced over all of the area to be covered.

Beware of having too much paint on the brush as it will make the paint spatters too large.

Repeat until the desired shading effect is obtained. More than one color may be used for a decorative affect.

Allow the paint to dry before handling the material.

If paint in pressure spray cans is used, pin the plant material tightly to the paper, fabric, or cork being printed, so that it will remain in place, and not be moved by the force of the spray. If possible, place the material in a vertical position for the pressure sprays work best when held upright. Doing the spraying inside a large cardboard carton will protect the adjacent areas.

Spray lightly, holding the spray can about 15 inches from the material. The area closest to the leaf or other plant material, may be sprayed more heavily if desired. Several colors may be used on a design. Metallic paints are especially effective.

Small tin cans of various sizes and shapes can be made into holders for pencils, paper clips, and other objects, by covering the outsides with the material on which the design has been sprayed. Attach with paste, mucilage, or rubber cement.

Leaves, grasses, and flowers may be arranged directly on the cans or boxes and sprayed with the paint, too. Let them dry thoroughly before handling.

After the paint is dry, a fixative, clear lacquer, shellac, or sealer may be applied to the surface. This will help keep the surfaces from becoming soiled.

BLOCK PRINTS

Leaves and grasses are better for this type of print than are flowers or entire plants. Try the tougher leaves which are more durable and can be used for several prints. The summer and fall leaves are the toughest and are better than tender spring leaves for printing in this manner for both the outline and the veining will show up very well. This type of print may take a bit longer to do than some of the other types but can be most effective. It can also be used satisfactorily on fabrics.

Block prints are excellent for recording and indentifying leaves.

USES:

Cover decorations for notebooks or record books

A record of leaves collected and identified

Christmas card decorations

Notepaper

Gift wrapping paper

Book or folder covers

Place-mats, coasters, and desk sets

Scarves, napkins, aprons, skirts, neckties

MATERIALS:

Block printing inks, artists' oil paints, or printer's ink

Piece of glass about 8" X 10" or larger; linoleum; or cookie
   sheet on which to roll out paint

Rubber roller (brayer) - it is best to have two or more,
   keeping one clean of paint

Pieces of scrap paper or newspaper

Pad of newspapers on which to work

Small tweezers for handling inked materials

Paper, fabric, or cork for printing -
   An unglazed paper takes the paint best, although a glossy
   paper can be printed. A glossy surface requires a much
   longer drying time and the prints will smudge more
   easily.

Light colored, smooth fabrics are best for the beginner to
   handle. Fabrics with a soluble sizing or finish should
   be washed before printing. Silks and synthetic fabrics
   take prints very well.

Cork may be finished with a fixative, clear shellac, lacquer,
   or sealer after the paint or ink is dry. This also makes
   the cork less absorbent and less likely to stain or soil.

HOW TO MAKE:

Plan a pleasing arrangement of the plant materials to be used.

Put a small amount of paint or ink on the rolling out surface
   (glass etc.). If oil colors are used from a tube, about
   one half inch squeezed from the tube should be sufficient.
   The rolling out surface should be large enough to permit
   rather extensive rolling of the paint or ink. If colors
   are to be blended, do this before rolling out the paint or
   ink.

Using a very light pressure on the roller, roll the paint in
several directions until it is smooth and the roller has
a light even coating.

Place a leaf, veined side up on a piece of scrap paper. Run
the roller over the leaf, giving it a light but even coat
of the paint or ink. Only the veins and margins will take
the paint if this is done correctly.

Pick up the inked leaf with tweezers, and place it, inked side
down, on the exact spot planned for the print.

Cover the leaf with a clean scrap of paper and roll across
it with the clean roller and a light but even pressure.
Once across is usually sufficient. Be most careful not
to move the leaf during rolling for this will result in
smudged outlines, and sometimes double veins and stems.
(Another way to make the final leaf print, is to cover it
with a small wood block, then hammer or press it firmly
on the material being printed.)

Remove the paper and leaf and there should be a good print.

Repeat the process if more than one print is needed to complete the design, making only one print at a time. Be
careful not to smudge the previous print.

Let paint or ink dry for several hours before handling. Block
prints on fabrics should dry for 24 hours. Then place
the print side down on absorbent paper or old cloth and
press with a warm iron. A cloth, wet with white vinegar,
may be used in pressing to help set the color. Fabrics
printed in this way may be carefully hand laundered.

PRINTING WITH A WOODEN BLOCK

Leaves and grasses with well defined and firm textures, may
be cemented to a wooden block and printed in the same man
ner as a regular linoleum block print. Pine needles are especially effective printed in this manner.

This method of printing almost always shows the background
impression of the wooden block. However, the design may
be planned so that this adds to the effect rather than detract-
ing from the final result.

USES:

Decorative for such things as Christmas or greeting cards,
or for gift wrapping paper.

MATERIALS:

Pine or other needles; durable leaves; etc.

Household or model cement

Small wood blocks

Material to be printed, usually paper but may be fabric

Mallet or hammer

Pad of newspapers

Block printing ink or artists' oil colors

Piece of glass about 8" X 10" or larger; linoleum; or cookie sheet on which to roll out paint or inks.

Rubber roller or brayer

HOW TO MAKE:

Cement the selected materials in a pleasing design on the wood block and let dry well before using.

Roll out inks or paint according to the directions in the previous section under "Block Prints".

Transfer the ink or paint to the material on the prepared block, either by rolling the paint on the material, or by pressing the prepared block directly into the rolled out paint.

Place the inked or painted block on the material to be printed, placed on a pad of newspapers, and pound the wood block with hammer or mallet. Or the material may be placed on a pad of newspapers on the floor, the block put into and stepped on with an even distribution of weight. This usually results in a good clear print.

RUB PRINTING

Here is still another way in which leaf prints may be made. It is very simple, yet effective.

USES:

Decoration on notepaper or cards

As a record of leaves collected and identified

MATERIALS:

Cotton

Graphite or colored chalk

Rubber roller (Brayer)

Paper to be printed

Fixative (from any art supply store)

Newspapers

HOW TO MAKE:

Using a small piece of cotton, rub either graphite or pow-
    dered colored chalk on the veined side of a leaf.

Place the paper to be printed, on a pad of newspapers, and
    lay the leaf with the chalked or graphited side down on
    the exact spot for the print. Cover with a piece of news-
    paper and roll carefully to transfer the color to the
    paper.

Lift the leaf from the paper and spray the leaf print with fix-
    ative to prevent smudging.

PLASTER CASTING A LEAF

A plaster cast of a leaf or flower makes an effective plaque
or paper-weight. It may be colored with water colors if
desired.

USES:

As a decoration or wall hanging

As a paperweight

For collection and identification purposes

MATERIALS

Plaster of Paris

Shallow dish or saucer

Stirring spoon or small stick

Paper clip

Water colors

Leaves or flowers to be cast

Vaseline or other grease

HOW TO MAKE:

Mix about one cupful of Plaster of Paris to the consistency
of heavy cream. Pour this into a shallow dish or saucer.

Press a paper clip into one edge of the plaster with the end
of the clip extending from the plaster far enough to form
a loop for hanging the completed plaque. The spot where
the paper clip is attached will form the top of the plaque.

Select a leaf or flower to be printed and grease the veined
side with vaseline.

Place the greased side on the surface of the plaster and press
lightly and evenly, just enough to make a light impression
in the plaster.

Set the saucer aside until the plaster has set. This should
take about one hour. When the plaster has hardened sufficiently, remove the leaf or flower and allow the plaster
to cure for at least twenty-four hours after which time,
the cast may be colored using water colors. If the cast
is not sufficiently cured, the water colors will soak into
the still moist plaster.

DYE PRINTING

Using powdered water colors or powdered dyes, effective
prints can be made on absorbent material. They may combine two or more colors.

USES:

Nature books or collections

Room decorations appliqued to various articles

Notebook covers

Greeting cards

Place cards

MATERIALS:

Leaves or flowers to be printed

Powdered water colors or dyes

Small brush - one for each color to be used

Paper towels, thin white blotters, or cloth to be printed

Rubber roller (Brayer)

Scissors

Paste

Construction paper or other material for mounting

HOW TO MAKE:

Select a leaf or flower and place it on a piece of scrap paper;
veined side up. Using a small dry brush, cover the leaf
with the powdered paint or dye. Brush the paint or dye
well onto the entire leaf. When the surface is covered,
shake off all excess paint or dye.

Moisten a paper towel with water and lay it on a flat surface.
Lay a dry paper towel over the moist one, and lay a
magazine or other light weight on the top to bring both
towels in good contact. Let this stand for 5 - 10 minutes
until excess moisture is absorbed.

Place the painted leaf on a newspaper pad with the veined side
up, and place the moist paper towel over the leaf. Roll
with the rubber roller or brayer. The print will be found
on the underside of the moist paper towel. Allow this
to dry well after which the print may be trimmed and
mounted on construction paper or in a notebook, or used
as an appliqued decoration.

Thin blotters may be used in place of the paper towels, or if
cloth is to be printed, commercial dyes should be used.

For two or more colors, simply use different colored paints
or dyes on the appropriate parts of the leaves or flowers,
matching the natural colors in as far as possible.

LEAF SKELETONS

SKELETONIZING A LEAF

Pounding away the fleshy parts of a leaf with a fine bristled brush leaves a skeleton of veins and rib, standing out in great detail. The fleshy parts are those which contain chlorophyl, and where carbon dioxide and water are brought together to form sugar. The veins and rib of the leaf are the lifelines which carry food to other parts of the plant.

USES:

Decorative

Educational

MATERIALS:

Fresh green leaves

Hair brush or shoe brush containing animal bristles. The bristles should be fine but not stiff. Synthetic bristles are too hard.

Pounding board - a piece of old carpeting tacked to a wooden backing.

HOW TO MAKE:

Place the leaf on the pounding board with the veined side down.

Hold the leaf firmly with one hand, tapping gently with the brush until the fleshy parts of the leaf are worn away, and only the skeleton remains.

Turn the leaf over occasionally and work on the underside.

Within ten or fifteen minutes there should be definite signs of progress.

To preserve leaf skeletons. cement them in a scrapbook, using a dark background, and cover with cellophane or clear plastic; or mount between pieces of plastic or glass.

NATURE PLAQUES

The woods and fields are full of the materials for making nature plaques having great charm. Applying basic elements of design to the wide variety of materials available, provides unlimited possibilities for creative activity.

USES:

Nature plaques are decorative and can be arranged singly or in groups on the walls of the home. They are particularly effective against plain backgrounds.

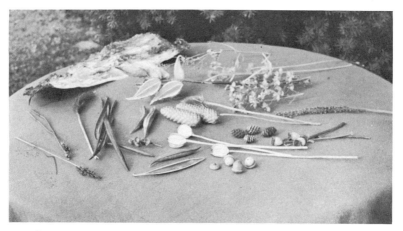

Raw materials of nature crafts include such things as birch bark, dried seed pods, cones, acorns, and grasses.

MATERIALS

Old boards, shingles, plywood, etc. for the background. A weathered effect is often desirable, but on occasion, a glossy waxed, varnished, or even painted finish makes an excellent background. The thin boards, used as backing in old picture frames, are very desirable for nature plaques. The plaques may be framed or left unframed as desired.

Household cement

Heavy shears or pruning shears

Tweezers

Clear lacquer, shellac, or spray plastic for the finished
   plaque if desired.

Native materials such as those listed below. The reader is
   certain to find many others which are not listed, and
   which are equally useful.

Nuts and cones of all kinds and sizes

Dried foliage of

   Beech
   Laurel
   Magnolia
   Mullen
   Oak
   Rhododendron

Dried branches of

   Baby's Breath
   Dogwood
   Larch
   Oak with acorns attached
   Witch-hazel

Dried flowers such as

   Pearly Everlasting
   Strawflowers
   Tansy

Cat-Tails

Dried Grasses

Driftwood

Dried Fungi

Lichens

Mosses

Seeds of

   Bayberry
   Beans
   Corn
   Grains
   Peas

Sunflowers
Vegetables
Fruits

Seed pods of

Alder
Ash
Beechnut
Catalpa
Day Lily
Gas Plant
Gladiolus
Lilac
Locust
Mallow
Maple
Milkweed
Morning Glory
Narcissus
Okra
Peony
Poppy
Siberian Lily
Teasel
Trumpet Vine
Tulip
Weeds
Witch-hazel
Yucca

Spike shapes such as catalpa seed pods, cat-tails, fern fronds, grasses, sensitive fern, and others may be used at the sides and tops of arrangements.

Ovals such as cones, some seed pods, etc., may be used at the base and towards the center of the composition.

Smaller forms may be used in a line arrangement to give the same effect as a spike.

Distinctive forms such as milkweed pods and okra pods give an interesting line and texture.

Indistinct forms such as baby's breath, mosses, and lichens may be used to fill in, or to "tie together" the more distinctive parts of the arrangement.

Plaque at the left is made of millet, azalea seed pods, sensitive fern spore fronds, poppy seed pods, dried lichens, velvety fungus, and dried weeds. Plaque at right is made of seeds and pits cemented to a sandpaper background. The basket is made of poppy seeds.

HOW TO MAKE:

Collecting the materials for "Nature Plaques" can be a year-round hobby, but for the best color and the most lasting qualities, materials should be gathered in the late fall or early winter after the first hard frosts. Every hike in the woods and fields, at any time of year, will turn up promising materials, however. Keep watch for the seed pods as they ripen on weeds and vines, and in the flower garden.

A few small boxes, one for each kind of material found, makes them readily available when needed.

Some seeds, such as acorns, are desirable in all stages of development, from the smallest to the fully developed sizes. Dry them carefully and store in a dry place to prevent mildew.

Cross-sections of pine, hemlock, and spruce cones look like roses, but the cross-sections may be difficult to cut. Try using a sharp chisel and mallet; coping saw, or heavy shears. Cross-sections of many seed pods also have striking designs. Cut them with a sharp knife or razor blade. In fact, many of the native materials found may be cut, or opened, or combined to form new and interesting designs.

Select and prepare the background to be used for the plaque.
A well weathered board may require no preparation.
Other backgrounds may need sanding, shellac, paint,
or perhaps a frame.

Decide on the basic design for the completed arrangement.
This design may be oval, crescent, V-shaped, L-shaped,
or may be in the shape of a triangle, fan, diagonal, or
S-shaped, and will partly depend upon the materials
being used and the natural shape of the larger pieces.
Branches, driftwood, cones, and seed-pods often give
an indication of the basic design to be followed.

Lay out the selected materials on a sheet of paper or cardboard of the same size as the background board to be
used. Place the larger materials first in the general
shape of the design selected. These are usually the outside or spike forms. Fill in with smaller materials
towards the center of the design and the focal point of
interest. Work in general from the top towards the
bottom of the plaque, and from the outside towards the
inside. The heavier parts of the plaque should be towards
the bottom or sides, and the lighter, more airy parts,
towards the top.

Some of the basic designs are illustrated.

Keep in mind the balance and proportion of the finished plaque,
building up the skeleton of the design first with the larger
pieces of native materials, and filling in the smaller de-
tails afterwards.

When the design is completely laid out on paper to your satisfaction, move the materials, one piece at a time to the
final background, cementing each piece in place. When
necessary, allow the cement to dry before adding more
materials.

Beware of using too much cement. A very small amount,
placed on the piece of material to be cemented to the
background, at each point of contact, is sufficient. Too
much cement may result in unsightly spots on the plaque.

When the cement is thoroughly dried, a finish such as shellac,
lacquer, or paint may be applied if desired. If individual
pieces are to be colored, this should be done before they
are cemented to the plaque. Be sure that the finish is
dry, before they are cemented. Such coloring may be
used to highlight parts of the plaque. Occasionally a
plaque may be sprayed with color or metallic paints.

FOUR BASIC DESIGNS
OF
NATURE PLAQUES

V - SHAPE

This plaque illustrates the V-shape of basic designs. It is made of driftwood, milkweed seed pods, trumpet-vine seed pods, cut hemlock cones, acorns, azalea seed pods, and parts of the seed balls of the sycamore tree.

L - SHAPE

CRESCENT

OVAL

Plaque made of cut shells cemented to a
stained background of textured plywood.

Place cards and plaque made of colored shells cemented to background.

DRIED FLOWERS

DRYING FLOWERS IN BORAX

Summer flowers live for only a few days, yet it is possible to keep them in all their beauty by following an old technique of dehydrating them in borax; a process which preserves color and texture, and in some cases, even the perfume.

USES:

Dried flowers may be used throughout the winter in flower arrangements, or in nature pictures; in glass paper-weights; in glass covered trays; or mounted in notebooks.

Cement a small dried flower to the top of a sheet of notepaper in a letter to a special friend.

MATERIALS:

Fresh flowers, picked just before the peak of bloom

Borax

Small cardboard box, depending on the amount of work to be done

Small plastic bags (freezer bags are excellent)

Florist's wire and green or brown florist's tape

Scissors

Cord

HOW TO MAKE:

Remove the stems, which do not dry well, from the flowers, then make a new stem of florist's wire, running it through the base of the flower and twisting the two ends together to form a stem.

Pour about one inch of borax in a plastic bag and place a flower face down in the borax. Add enough borax to cover the flower to a depth of about one inch. More flowers and more borax may be added until the bag is almost full. Carefully gather the top of the bag, squeeze out the remaining air, and tie with cord.

Place several bags of flowers and borax in a cardboard box and put in a dry place for at least four weeks. The flowers may then be carefully removed from the borax, dusted off, and used in flower arrangements. The wire stems may then be wound with either green or brown florist's tape.

Try this method of drying flowers on such varieties as dogwood, marigolds, chrysanthemums, pansies, single roses, sweetpeas, and zinnias. You'll like it.

SUN-BAKED FLOWERS

The same varieties of flowers that dry well in borax, may also be dried by baking in sand in the sun.

MATERIALS:

Flowers cut at the peak of bloom

Fine dry sand

Flour sifter or fine sieve

Shallow cardboard box

HOW TO MAKE:

Sift fine dry sand to remove all coarse particles

Remove all leaves from the stems of the flowers

Pour one to two inches of sand in a shallow cardboard box, then place the flowers gently upside down on the sand, carefully pouring more sand over each flower to cover to a depth of about one inch. The stems need not be covered. Leave ample space between flowers so they do not touch.

Place the box of sand and flowers in the sun to bake. If the weather is dry and hot, two or three days will be ample. When thoroughly dry, carefully pour off the sand, and use a small paint brush if necessary, to remove particles of sand sticking to the flowers.

In making flower arrangements, use dried materials such as baby's breath, or evergreen twigs, to replace the leaves removed from the flowers.

PRESERVING FOLIAGES WITH GLYCERINE

Foliages of beach, oak, maple, holly, and similar varieties may be preserved using glycerine. It does not work too well on flowers, however.

USES:

Preserved foliages are excellent in arrangements of dried flowers, and for winter bouquets. They may also be used with fresh flowers.

MATERIALS:

Foliage gathered early in the morning.

Hammer

Jar containing two parts water and one part glycerine with
the liquid at least three inches deep.

HOW TO MAKE:

Remove all defective leaves from the foliage and pound the
lower two inches of the stems with a hammer or mallet,
crushing and splitting the stems to aid absorption of the
water and glycerine solution.

Stand the stems in the solution to a depth of at least three
inches and set the jar aside until the glycerine is fully
absorbed into the leaves. This may take anywhere from
three or four days to two weeks. The glycerine is fully
absorbed when the leaves take on a glossy effect.

Leaves of some plants may also be preserved by this method,
especially ivy leaves, using a solution of equal parts of
water and glycerine.

Foliages preserved in glycerine normally last for months and
even years.

Any glycerine solution remaining may be saved and used
again.

PRESSING LEAVES AND FLOWERS

Pressing is another method of drying leaves, grasses, and
some flowers for winter use. It works well with nearly all
leaves of trees, and with Queen Anne's Lace, sweet clover,
grasses such as foxtail, timothy, June grass, rose leaves,
sumac, cinquefoil, pearly everlasting flowers and many
others. Green ferns, and ferns that have turned brown or
yellow, are very beautiful when pressed. Use the methods
outlined below, or build the "Leaf Press" described on the
pages following this article.

USES:

Lampshades - dried plant materials cemented to either outside or inside of transparent or translucent shade.

Wall decorations as framed pictures, tiles, or plaques

Paper weights in the form of arrangements on the insides of hollow glass paperweights.

Winter bouquets

MATERIALS:

Absorbent paper - blotters, newspapers, or paper towels

Paper for mounting the dried materials

Fiberglass, plastic, or parchment for covering lampshade frames

Household cement or rubber cement

Plastic spray

HOW TO MAKE:

Gather leaves, ferns, grasses, etc., preferably those that are rather flat in form. Late summer or fall is a good time for gathering materials as they are then beginning to dry naturally. Place them between sheets of absorbent paper under a weight. Leave them for several days in a dry place, changing the absorbent paper occasionally to provide for thorough drying.

When they seem to be thoroughly dry, store them between pieces of paper or in leaves of an old book to prevent damage.

When mounting dried materials on a lampshade or other article, spread a quick-drying adhesive on the spot selected for the design; then press the leaves or other materials into the adhesive and allow to dry. After everything is dry, spray the entire surface with a clear plastic spray or fixative. More than one coat of spray may be needed to give a finished look, and to protect the surface of the plant materials. Too many coats may give an undesirable slick or glossy appearance.

A new lampshade may be made from an old one by removing the old covering, leaving the wire frame and recovering this with plastic, fiberglass, or parchment. Make a pattern by placing the wire frame at the edge of a sheet of heavy wrapping paper. Roll the wire frame across the wrapping paper carefully marking the track of the frame with a pencil, both at the top and bottom edges of the frame.

Cut out this paper pattern, using it as a pattern for marking
and cutting a new shade from the material selected.
Some of these transparent or translucent materials may
be found under the names of "Clearophane", "Clearo-
film", "Synskin", and others.

Using a leather punch, punch holes 1/8 inch in diameter, one
inch apart, and about 3/16 inch in from all edges of the
material. Lace to the wire frame with raffia, Basswood
(Indian) cordage, colored twine, or yarn.

MAKING A LEAF PRESS

Colored fall leaves, and other leaves and plants are often
pressed and when dried may be used in arrangements of
flowers and other native materials.

An effective press for drying leaves and plants is easily made
and may be carried on field trips where the collected materials may be placed in the press immediately.

MATERIALS:

2 pieces of 1/4 inch plywood - 12" X 15"

6 pieces of 1/4 inch lumber - 4" X 12" for braces

2 carriage bolts - 3/8" X 2" with wing-nuts

2 washers 3/8" hole

2 pieces of leather or rope for handles, about 12" long

48 screws - 1/2" long

20 blotters - 12" X 15"

Model cement

HOW TO MAKE:

Two covers or press boards are made according to the following directions and illustration at top of the next page.

Braces are screwed to each edge and one diagonal of each of
the 12" X 15" pieces of plywood, and 3/8" holes drilled
for the bolts at the center of each of the outside braces,
making certain that the holes in the opposite sides coin-
cide.

The bolts are place through the holes in one of the covers
and the bolt heads cemented in place. Washers are

34

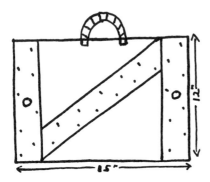

Dimensional drawing of one of two sides of leaf press. Winged nuts at each side press plant materials between sheets of white blotter paper in the press.

cemented over the holes in the opposite cover, on the outside, leaving the smooth sides of the covers for the insides of the leaf press.

Holes are punched or cut in the blotters to fit over the bolts.

Handles are attached by tacking or screwing one to the outside of each cover.

Sassafras leaves have been dried in this leaf press.

TO USE:

The wing-nuts are removed and the leaf or other plant material to be pressed is placed between two of the sheets of
blotter paper. The cover is then replaced and the wing-
nuts tightened.

The material will dry flat, but should be moved on the blotters occasionally so that moisture is more quickly absorbed.

WINTER BOUQUETS

During late summer and early fall, gardens and fields provide a wide variety of materials for making winter bouquets.
Dried weeds, seed-pods, corn-stalks, grains, leaves and
branches are useful. Collect those having interesting textures and shapes and have them ready for use when the color
of summer and fall is replaced by the drabness of winter.

MATERIALS:

Bittersweet

Blonde corn tassels

Catalpa pods

Cat-tails, picked and dried
before ripening, or with
the fluff removed.

Cones

Curly dock

Fern fronds or fern spore-
stalks

Goldenrod

Gourds

Grape leaves

Grasses

Magnolia leaves

Milkweed stems and pods

Okra pods

Osage oranges

Palm boots

Rhododendron leaves

Sprays of millet

Sprays of wheat

Sprays of rye or barley

Teasel	Witch-hazel branches
Thistles	Yarrow
Trumpet Vine seed-pods	Yucca

HOW TO MAKE:

Effective winter bouquets are the result of both selection of materials and good arrangement; an art that many of us do not easily come by.

Try some of these:

Combine a few blonde corn-tassels with the brown of cat-tails or curly dock. Place a figurine in the foreground. Arrangements may be held in place by "frogs" purchased from any flower shop, or they may be pushed into a block of styrofoam. Try covering the styrofoam with burlap or crepe paper and pushing the stems through the covering into the plastic foam.

Try a flat tray or basket arrangement with an osage orange, yarrow, or thistle flowers towards the front, and with cat-tails, wheat, corn tassels, or corn-stalks, and heavier, taller native materials at the back.

Try covering a piece of wallboard or plywood with green burlap, and add a spray of golden wheat with highlights of gold or bronze spray paint. Tie with a brown ribbon and add a few bittersweet berries.

Pewter and copper vases; brown or green earthenware bowls; and other simple types of vases and jars are excellent for winter bouquets.

For most effective use, smaller materials such as cones, osage oranges, seed pods, etc., may be wired to hold them in place. Twist heavy florist's wire, or any soft iron wire such as "stovepipe wire", around the base of the materials. Wrap the wire with florist's tape wherever it may show in the finished arrangement. The wire may then be twisted around wooden "picks" for pushing into a styrofoam base, or the wires themselves may be twisted and pushed into the styrofoam.

Most household magazines show suggested arrangements from which you may plan your own from the materials at hand.

ARRANGEMENTS UNDER GLASS

ROSE BOWLS OR GLASS DOMES

Beautiful arrangements of twigs, grasses, milkweed pods, ferns, cones, poppy seedpods, teasel, and berries, can be made under rose bowls or glass domes available at most florists. Variations in line, shape, and color show up well. Foam plastic such as styrofoam, or modeling clay, may be used as a base to hold the arrangement in place.

Glass domes are available with screw bases, or clear glass jars with screw tops may be inverted and used. A bubble bowl, usually used to float a single flower in water, may be inverted on a plastic or other base and make a good cover for an arrangement.

Since this type of arrangement can be viewed from all sides, the taller materials should be used in the center, and shorter materials around the sides.

Those using the native materials should be encouraged to learn the names of the plant materials used; where it may be found; and its place in nature as well as in camp or in the home.

PAPER WEIGHTS

Hollow-backed paper weights in various shapes and sizes are available from craft supply stores, paper stores, and souvenir shops. Some may be dome shaped and will magnify. Others are flat with recessed backs.

These are all excellent for using in craft projects, and will show new and surprising colors, shapes, and textures in common plant materials. You will find them absorbing, and with most satisfying results.

Because the materials used must necessarily be small, it takes time and patience to arrange them, and a rather delicate touch is needed. Very young children and impatient adults may not be patient enough. However they may enjoy using the tiny cones, acorns, berries, grasses, seeds, twigs, fungi, etc. for the simple arrangements.

Here again, the exact directions cannot be given for making the designs or for the plant materials to use, so a few examples will be given.

MATERIALS:

Plant materials - small and thoroughly dried

Plain glass magnifying paperweights or flat paperweights,
    rectangular or round, and which do not magnify

Cardboard, cork, birchbark, or fabric for the background

Household cement

Tweezers and toothpicks

HOW TO MAKE:

Draw around the base of the paperweight on paper or card-
    board. Cut out this pattern to be used in planning and
    trying out the arrangement.

Decide on the background to be used - paper, cardboard,
    cork, or bark and cut it to the size of the pattern. If it

is light weight, cement it to a heavier piece of cardboard cut to the same size.

Make the arrangement piece by piece, using tweezers or toothpicks to put the tiny materials in place. After putting each piece in place, set the paperweight over the design, making certain that it looks well before adding another piece of material.

After the arrangement is planned, cement each piece carefully to the selected background material. Cement it securely, but be careful not to have excess cement which may show as shiny spots in the arrangement. Cement may be placed on the tiny plant materials with the tip of a toothpick.

When the arrangement is completed, put cement on the base of the glass paperweight and carefully set it over the finished arrangement. Let it dry well before handling.

Since this type of paper weight magnifies, materials used in arrangements must be very small and carefully arranged in a small recess in the back of the paper weight.

EXAMPLES:

One arrangement might show several kinds of ferns and grasses arranged on a base of white birchbark. Another could be made of a single milkweed floss, a tiny twig of bayberry, everlasting flowers, and a ruffled fungus of velvety green or rust color. Still another might have a variety of tiny acorns, seeds, and berries, sensitive-fern spores, bittersweet, lilac seed pods, witch-hazel, cedar seed pods, and red stemmed dogwood arranged on a cork background. Others might show collections of minerals, colorful bits of butterfly wings, or other materials.

NATURE COSTUME JEWELRY

This is a group of small "nature craft" articles that are
unique. They are fascinating to "dream up" and can be made
for personal use or as gifts. Children and grown-ups alike
enjoy collecting and experimenting with materials to make
really beautiful articles. Since these materials are often
very small, it requires patience and some manual dexterity
to achieve satisfactory results. Perhaps it requires a certain type of person, too, who has a liking for fine work. Try
some of the following things and see what you can create for
yourself.

Earrings   Pins and Pendants   Boutonnieres

These can well be made during the fall and winter, as well
as in the summer, for the materials used should be thoroughly dried. Tiny bits and pieces of plant material assume
a new importance when planning the design of an earring,
for example. Most of the plant materials listed at the beginning of this book can be used, either whole or in sections.
A good example is the teasel. It is much too large for an
earring or a pin, but the tiny spurs when separated from the
rest of the head, may have just the right line and color to
complete a tiny design.

Collect, sort, and keep materials for these small crafts in
small paper or plastic boxes. Other supplies are inexpensive
and fairly easy to obtain.

Exact directions cannot be given here for the best results
are those "invented" as you work. A few examples may be
of the most help.

EARRINGS, PINS, PENDANTS

MATERIALS:

All kinds of dried plant materials - seeds, cones, flowers,
    berries

Tiny shells (shells may also be purchased cut into sections

Backing for the arrangements - cork, plastic, wood, or
    bamboo

Earring backs and pin backs of
  metal or plastic (purchased
  from craft supply stores)

Household or model cement

Plastic spray or clear lacquer

Sequins, beads, glitter (if desired)

Tweezers or toothpicks for
  manipulating small pieces

HOW TO MAKE:

The following examples are
  typical of the possibilities:

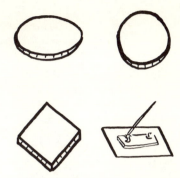

Plastic and other backings for pins
and pendants come in various shapes.
Pin-backs or earring-backs may be
cemented to the backing after the
arrangement has been cemented
to the front.

    1. Acorn cups make fine ear-
rings. Select two that are
similar in size, shape, and
color. Sand or file the
stem end until it is flat and
smooth enough to fit on the earring backing. Cement
the acorn cups to the earrings, using a generous
amount of cement. Let this dry thoroughly before
proceeding farther.

    Inside the acorn cup, cement an arrangement of ber-
ries, seeds, tiny cones, or flowers. Plan the design
before cementing the pieces. Use cement sparingly,
placing it on the material being cemented with a toothpick. Use the tweezers to put the materials in place.

    2. Cut two pieces of cork in round, square or other
desired shape of a desirable size for an earring.
With these as a base, make an arrangement of tiny
seeds, seed pods, etc. Sequins and beads may be
added for a bit of sparkle. A small child might
cement a circle of sunflower seeds around a tiny
acorn cup or the tip of a small cone. Seed pods of
lilac are most interesting used singly with barberry
or bittersweet, or they may be grouped together
around a bead or sequin center.

    3. In the 5 & 10 cent stores, costume earrings may be
found having thin dangling metal hoops. These may
be used for the backing on which to cement an interesting arrangement of native materials. Small hemlock cones can be cemented inside the metal hoops,
or an acorn cup may be used to make an unusual
drop earring.

> 4. Thin wood, plastic or cork cut in various shapes
> may be used as the backgrounds for pins and pend-
> ant, with the size and shape depending on the fancy
> of the person making them.

Flat designs of lilac seed pods, pearly everlasting flowers
or bittersweet, barberries or bayberries, grasses or
grains can be very handsome. More bulky arrangements
of cones, acorns, and witch-hazel combined with berries,
etc., mat suit some designers better. Anyway that you
choose has unlimited possibilities.

After the arrangement is planned and cemented to the backing,
let it dry well and then cement a pin back in place. Let
this dry and it is ready to wear.

If a pendant is wanted, tiny metal jump-rings may be purchased from a craft supply house, put through a small
hole drilled or punched in the backing and closed with
pliers. A chain, cord, or leather thong may be used to
suspend the pendant. It is best to attach the jump-ring
to the backing before the arrangement of native materials
is cemented in place. Cork makes an especially nice
base or backing for pendants.

Slice or cut sections of shells, purchased from some craft
supply houses, make particularly interesting and beautiful earrings and other costume jewelry.

It is sometimes advisable, after the product is finished, to
spray it with a clear lacquer or plastic spray. This
helps to protect the surface and gives a bit of luster.
Most craftsman prefer a velvet or even a natural finish
to a shiny glossy appearance, however. A touch of met-
talic spray, or bronze applied with a small brush may
be tried also.

WINTER BOUTONNIERES

Plant materials that do not break or fall apart easily, can be
used in the making of boutonnieres for the winter holidays.
Stems are needed, but cones, acorns, and the like can be
provided with florist's wire stems, and used to add a variety
of shapes, colors, and textures.

Children like to make these for their mothers as well as for
themselves. They can also be used as favors on a holiday
table.

MATERIALS:

Dried plant materials of a durable nature such as cones,
     acorns, lilac seed pods, witch-hazel, etc.

Florist's wire - size 26 or 28

Florist's tape - green and brown

Pliers and wire cutters or household shears

Small Christmas bells, balls, sequins, and glitter

Ribbon - 1/2 inch width

Household cement

Clear and metallic spray paints

HOW TO MAKE:

Assemble short lengths of plant materials not more than
     4 - 6 inches

Cut florist's wire into 8 - 12 inch pieces

Wire each piece separately, making the stems stiff but plia-
     ble, by doubling a piece of florist's wire and wrapping
     in both directions for the full length of the stem, start-
     ing at the top of the stem.

Wire each cone, acorn, and berry by pushing a doubled wire
     through with the loop of the wire holding the material,
     and the two ends twisted to form a stem.

Wrap each individual wired stem with florist's tape. Start
     the tape just above the wired stem. Hold the tape tightly,
     twist the stem and stretch the tape as you twist so that
     it clings to the wire stem. A little practice will make
     this step go rapidly.

Assemble the wired and taped pieces into a desirable arrange-
     ment and wire all of the stems securely together. The
     wire stems will permit the materials to be easily ar-
     ranged by bending the stems.

Make a bow or use loops of ribbon to finish the boutonniere.
     Wire this tightly at the center and wrap the wire around
     the arrangement. Be sure that all wire is covered with
     florist's tape.

NATIVE DYES

While it is true that commercial dyes come in a greater
variety of colors and shades than dyes made from native materials, and are much more reliable and of a fast color,
there is still satisfaction and charm in making and using
native dyes. The materials for native dyes are easily obtained from the many plants, vegetables, fruits, and trees
which provide these materials.

USES:

Dying of cotton, woolen, linen, or rayon materials

MATERIALS:

Onion skins	- Red or yellow dye
Raspberries	- Dark red
Blood-root	- Red
Beets	- Red violet
Strawberries	- Red
Mountain Ash berries	- Orange
Goldenrod plant and flowers	- Yellow
Pear leaves	- Yellow (dull)
Sumac roots	- Yellow
Sumac leaves	- Yellow brown
Celladine	- Yellow
Tanglewood stems	- Yellow
Citron	- Yellow
Elderberry leaves	- Green
Rhubarb leaves	- Light green
Larkspur flowers	- Blue
Blackberries	- Blue
Pokeweed berries	- Purple
Dandelion roots	- Magenta

Sassafras roots	- Pink
Butternut bark	- Brown
Walnut hulls	- Rich dark brown
Sumac bark	- Brown

Also needed are an enamel kettle for boiling the materials, plus the material selected to be dyed.

HOW TO MAKE:

Experiment in making the various native dyes by soaking the materials in water overnight, and then boiling for an hour or more to give the desired intensity of color. Strain well to remove all plant materials before using the dyes.

Stems and barks used for native dyes should be gathered during the spring or early summer. Roots should be collected in the fall, and leaves just as they are reaching full growth in the late spring. Flowers are gathered at the peak of bloom, and berries and seeds when they are ripe.

NOTES ON THE PREPARATION OF VARIOUS DYES:

Goldenrod - chop the flowers and plant into small pieces. Add water and bring to a boil. Simmer for several hours and then cool. After about 24 hours, reheat, add the cloth to be dyed and let simmer until the desired color is obtained.

Pear leaves - pound the leaves to shreds and bring to a boil until the maximum color is obtained.

Berries and stems - boil in a very small amount of water for two hours. Strain well and add one part of wood alcohol to three parts of dye to keep from spoiling too quickly.

Barks and roots - boil for four to five hours in a small amount of water. Strain and add one tablespoon salt for each pint of dye.

Onion skins - boil in small amount of water for about two and one half hours. Add cloth to the strained dye and boil for one hour.

Most of the native dyes are fairly permanent and should be used while hot on dry materials.

DYEING:

Place sufficient water in an enamel kettle to cover the cloth
to be dyed. Add the concentrated dye to the water and
bring to a boil. Place the cloth in the dye bath. Dye
to the desired shade, remove, wring out and dry.

To make the dye fast, the material may be treated before
dyeing. To treat the cloth, make an alum bath, using
one ounce of alum to a gallon of water. For woolen
cloth, add 1/4 ounce of cream of tartar. For cotton,
linen, or rayon, add 1/4 ounce of washing soda. Boil
the cloth for at least an hour, rinse well, and dry before
placing it in the hot dye bath.

Try some of these dyes for tie-dyeing, or on unbleached
muslin to be used for craft purposes or for costuming.

GARDEN ON A BUTTON

Miniature living gardens, arranged and grown on a single button, are fun to make and will prove to be real conversation pieces.

MATERIALS:

Tiny cacti or other small succulants

Sand

Tweezers

Peat Moss

Household Cement

Large button, small coaster, or even a milk bottle cap

Tiny pebbles or shells

HOW TO MAKE:

Place a small amount of cement on a button and attach the tallest cacti or other succulant just off center. Cement two or three smaller cacti or succulants in place near the first. Let the cement dry for a few minutes and then cement a few small pebbles, shells, or carefully chosen pieces of crushed rock, leaving a little space between them for sand and peat moss.

Put small amounts of cement on the empty spaces on the button and sprinkle with clean sand, shaking off the excess sand. Using the tweezers, tuck tiny pieces of peat moss into the openings around the cacti and pebbles to hold moisture for the growing plants.

Adding a few drops of water about once each week will keep the button garden growing for months.

GROWING A CRYSTAL GARDEN

Among the most beautiful shapes found in nature are those which occur as crystals. These may be snowflakes, quartz, calcite, salt, fool's gold, or many others which are found in a wide variety of shapes and sizes.

Most of these crystals are formed where you cannot see the process but it is possible to set up your own crystal garden and actually watch the crystals grow.

USES:

As decorations and conversations pieces

As a means of learning how crystals are formed

MATERIALS:

Nut-sized pieces of soft coal, coke, or broken brick (the size and shape are not of particular importance)

4 tablespoons of common salt (not iodized)

4 tablespoons of liquid bluing

4 tablespoons of water

1 tablespoon of household ammonia

Medicine dropper

Food coloring, fabric dye, or other coloring material such as mercurochrome

6 inch dish

HOW TO MAKE:

Place several pieces of coal, coke, or brick in the dish. Arrange them near the center of the dish but do not have the pieces touching each other.

Mix in this order - salt, bluing, water, and ammonia stirring each as you go. The salt should dissolve in the water before the ammonia is added.

Pour the mixture very slowly over the broken pieces of coal, etc. in the dish. Add small spots of color with the med-icine dropper and dyes, rinsing the dropper between colors.

Crystals will begin to form within a short time, and in a few hours will take on interesting shapes, continuing their growth for several days.

Since the crystal garden will crumble easily, let it grow at the place where you wish to show it.

CHRISTMAS ORNAMENTS

In this particular article we will limit the suggestions to ideas for small ornaments for table or tree. The whole field of Christmas decorations is so large and varied that we will not try to cover it in a comprehensive way.

Children enjoy making oranments from nuts, cones, and milkweed pods, and there is plenty of scope for their imagination.

MATERIALS:

Cones of all sizes

Milkweed pods

Nuts - especially English walnuts

Household cement

Fine wire

Metallic Paints

Sequins and glitter

Copper "Choregirl"

HOW TO MAKE:

Here again, the most successful results come from experimenting, and giving the imagination free rein. The examples given here are only intended to start "genius burning", and are not meant to be limiting in any sense.

1. Milkweed pods are beautiful in shape and color. Wire together three of the same size and shape, at the stem ends, leaving enough wire for a hanging loop. In the hollow of each pod, cement a small Christmas ball; or cover the inside of the pod with cement and sprinkle sequins or glitter over the cement. The pods may be sprayed with one of the metallic paints if you wish, or may be painted with any bright color.

2. Spray a single milkweed pod with metallic paint or gilt. Cover it with a light coat of cement and sprinkle with glitter or sequins. If the slim center section of the milkweed pod is still in place, fasten

this more securely with cement and color or add sequins. This center section extends from end to end of the milkweed pod, and originally served to hold the milkweed floss and seeds in place. A wire may be added to the stem end for hanging, or several pods may be wired together in strings or clusters.

3. Teasel with its beautiful curving spines, may be sprayed or dipped in gold or silver paint, wired at the stem end, and hung on the Christmas Tree, or used in a table arrangement or a swag for the door.

4. Paint or gild whole English walnuts and decorate with sequins, tinsel, or glitter. Use half shells of walnuts as tiny shadow boxes, with tiny Christmas balls, bells, etc. cemented inside. Use small pieces of copper from a "Chore girl" inside the walnut halves as colorful background for sequin birds, stars, tiny trees, etc.

These ideas are only a beginning. See what you can do.

WEAVING WITH NATIVE MATERIALS

INDIAN MAT LOOM

The Indians of the southwest use a simple loom for making mats and rugs. This type of loom can easily be adapted for the making of place-mats and other simple articles of native materials. Although the Indians use this loom for making large mats and rugs, a much smaller loom may be made as described at the end of this article.

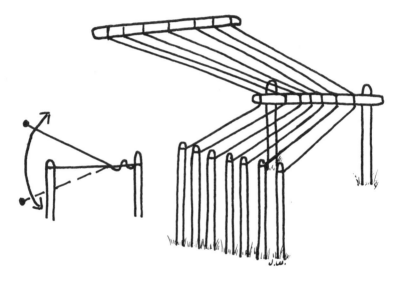

The large illustration shows the Indian Loom as it might be set up out-of-doors for weaving of heavier materials. The small illustration indicates the method of raising and lowering the moveable warp cords for the insertion of "woof" materials in the caves above and below the stationary warp cords.

MATERIALS:

Slender stakes or dowels to be driven into the ground, and to which the stationary warp coards are fastened. In the illustration we have seven of these plus one cross-piece. We also need one slender cross-piece to which the moveable warp cords are attached.

Warp cords - medium weight cords of various colors as desired. The width of the completed mat is determined
 by the number of stationery warp cords, and the distance
 of these cords apart.

Woof materials - these are the materials which are to be
 woven into a mat or rug, such as bunches of grass,
 straw, rushes, cat-tails, etc.

HOW TO MAKE:

A completed mat made of cat-
tails looks something like this.

Stakes are driven into the
 ground as shown in the diagram. The length of the
 mat or rug will be the same
 as the length of the stationary warp cords. The width
 will be just slightly more
 than the space between the
 outside warp cords. Drive
 the stakes into the ground
 according to the size of the
 mat which you wish to make.

The stationary warp cords are
 attached to the stakes and
 cross-piece as shown in the
 illustration. The cords
 should be parallel to each
 other, but do not need to be
 the same distance apart.
 Variations in spacing them
 apart will add interest to
 the finished mat.

The moveable warp cords are attached to the cross-piece at
 the same point as are the stationary warp cords. They
 are also fastened to a moveable cross-piece at the other
 ends of the cords, with the cords cut several inches
 longer than the stationary cords.

Grass, straw, or other "woof" materials are laid across the
 stationary warp cords in the V-shaped "cave" between
 the moveable and stationary warp cords. They are alternately placed above and below the stationary warp
 cords.

After each piece of material is laid across the stationary
 warp, the moveable warp is raised or lowered alternately
 on the right and left sides of the corresponding stationary

warp cords and the "woof" material placed across the
warp again. As each section of "woof" is put in place.
it should be pushed tightly against the previous section
of "woof".

When the mat has reached the desired length, the ends of
the warp cords are cut and tied and the edges of the
mat trimmed.

MAKING A SMALL INDIAN MAT LOOM

Using nine 1/4 inch dowels, each 5 inches long, and a shallow wooden or cardboard box, about 7 X 12 inches;
pour about 1" depth of Plaster of Paris into the box,
setting seven of the dowels upright across on end of
the box, and two more dowels upright at the opposite
corners of the box, (or set the dowels in a wooden base).

When the plaster has hardened, cement or lash an 8 inch
dowel across the tops of the two dowels at one end of
the box.

Tie warp threads between the tops of the seven dowels and
the cross piece; tie seven more warp threads at the
same points on the cross-piece, and to another 8 inch
dowel. This serves as the handle for the moveable
warp.

Weave according to previous directions.

WEAVING ON A CARDBOARD LOOM

A simple but effective loom can be made from a strong, flexible piece of cardboard. A piece of cardboard 15 X 20 inches
will make a table mat of about 14 X 18 inches in size.

USES:

A cardboard loom may be used with any of the common native materials used as "woof". The warp is made of
cotton twine or regular carpet thread. Metallic threads
add interest and color. This type of loom is particularly
effective in making table mats, using straw for the
"woof".

A small loom may be used in weaving place-mats.
Dried wheat straw is being used in this one.

A place-mat of wheat straw woven on the
Small Indian Mat Loom shown above.

MATERIALS:

A piece of strong flexible cardboard the width of the weaving
   to be made, and about two inches longer than the finished
   weaving is to be. Cotton twine, carpet warp, or other
   heavy cotton thread

Weaving materials such as straw, grasses, raffia, cat-tails,
   rushes, reeds, bark cordage, etc.

Pan of water (most materials are more flexible when kept
   moist)

HOW TO MAKE:

Make cuts, 1/4 inch deep, 1/2 inch apart across both ends
   of the cardboard, making certain that there is an uneven
   number of cuts on each end. These cuts are used to
   hold the warp threads.

Tie a knot in one end of a long double strand of thread, and
   slip the knot into the first cut in one end of the cardboard
   with the knot on the underside. Bring the threads down
   through the cut in the opposite end of the cardboard; up
   through the next cut and back across the front of the
   cardboard and down through the cut next to the knot.

Continue in this fashion until the loom is complete threaded
   with all of the warp threads going lengthwise on the
   front of the cardboard loom. Bring the warp threads
   across the back of the loom after they have gone through
   the last cut of the loom and tie to the beginning thread
   where it is knotted. This completes the threading of
   the loom.

WEAVING:

Straw and most other weaving materials should be soaked in
   water (overnight if possible) to make them flexible.

Weave the first straw across one end of the loom, between
   the double strands of warp. The next straw or weaver
   goes over one thread and under the next across the loom.
   The third straw also goes over and under the warp
   threads, but where the second straw went over, the
   third straw goes under, and vice versa.

The straws used as weavers should be pushed closely together
   each time one is added, and the warp threads should be
   kept parallel.

Continue weaving in straws and pushing them together until the mat reaches the end of the loom.

The tension is kept on the warp threads by the natural bending of the cardboard.

Patterns may be made by skipping some of the warp threads, or by cutting the slits in the ends of the loom closer together or farther apart, or by the use of different colored warp threads, or by using different materials for the weavers or "woof".

FINISHING THE WOVEN MAT:

Using a straight edge as a guide, cut the straws evenly, about one inch from the outside warp threads.

When the warp is filled, and the edges have been trimmed, add several rows of thread, woven lengthways through the ends of the straws to give added strength. Use double strands similar to the warp, and several inches longer than the length of the mat.

Slip the warp threads from the slits of the cardboard loom, and weave additional straws through the loose warp ends making the mat firm.

CORDAGE

INDIAN CORDAGE

The bark and roots of certain trees, shrubs, and weeds, provided the Indians with the materials for making cordage for lacings, rope, and fishlines. These materials are also useful in the nature crafts program, and a knowledge of how they are made adds interest which on occasion may be very useful.

Some of the plants and trees from which cordage may be made are listed here.

Basswood	- Inner bark
Leatherwood	- Strands of split bark
Hemlock	- Small root fibers
Spruce	- Rootlets
Larch	- Small root fibers
Indian Hemp	- Shredded bark fibers
Milkweed	- Shredded fibers
Elm	- Inner bark
White Oak	- Inner bark
Red Cedar	- Inner bark
Black Locust	- Inner bark

USES:

Cordage made from the above materials may be used for fishlines; for lacing in craft projects (similar to raffia); and may even be made into rope. A quarter inch rope made of basswood bark is considerably stronger than a manila rope of the same size, if properly made. Cordage may also be used in weaving.

HOW TO MAKE:

Each kind of cordage is made in a similar manner once the fibers are obtained and made ready for use. Root fibers are ready to use when the bark has been removed from them. Indian hemp and milkweed need only be shredded into long fibers, using only the mature plants. Soaking and gentle pounding usually helps to separate the fibers.

Most of the barks are prepared in the same manner. This
manner will be illustrated using Basswood which is the
best source of cordage in the Northeast, and is very
strong when properly prepared. In other sections of
the country, other barks or plants may be more readily
available.

To prepare basswood bark, strip it from the tree in pieces
of five feet or more in length. Put these to soak in
small pond or lake (still water) for from 10 to 30 days.
These will partially rot, a process called "retting" and
the thin strands of the inner bark are easily removed
after this prolonged soaking. Pounding the bark with a
wooden mallet on a block of wood helps to separate the
fibers into paper-thin strips that are very pliable. Wash
Wash these strands well and hang them up to dry.

If you wish better materials, boil the separated fibers for
2 - 3 hours in a container with a few handfuls of wood
ashes, then wash the fibers well before drying. The
wood ashes contain a weak solution of lye.

The basswood fibers may be used "as is" or may be dyed any
desirable color with any good fabric dyes, or you may
wish to make your own dyes from native materials as
described elsewhere in this book.

Always soak the bark fibers well before using them, making
them more pliable.

MAKING CORDAGE:

Take two long thin strands; lay them across the thigh, rolling
them together with the palm of the right hand in one direction, twisting them together into a round twine. Pull
the twine out with the left hand as each section is twisted
and continue rolling until near the end of the strands.
Cut one strand a few inches shorter than the other and
lay a new strand against the shorter piece and continue
rolling.

A stronger cordage may be made by taking two rolled strands
(or a single strand doubled), and twisting the two strands
in the opposite directions from that in which they have
been rolled.

This is done as follows: (See illustration): Take two rolled
strands and tie them at one end; or take a doubled strand
and hang it over a nail, about one foot from the center
of the strand. This is to make the ends uneven for the
adding of additional strands.

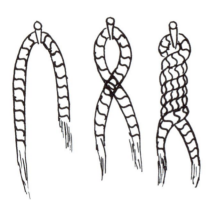

Take one end in each hand just below the nail, twist the strands from left to right, tightening them in the same direction as they were originally rolled. As the strands are rolled tight, twist the two strands together in the opposite direction to that which they have been rolled. Thus the two single strands are twisted in one direction, and then the single strands are twisted together in the opposite direction, preventing them from coming untwisted. Continue this process until the cordage is as long as is desired. Just before the end of the shorter strand is reached, lay another strand of equal size against it and continue the process. Keep the bark wet while working.

Method of making cordage from a single strand of rolled bark.

When the desired length is reached, stretch and dry the rope between two bent saplings or with weights at the ends, to hold the cordage taut while drying. When thoroughly dry (about 48 hours) trim off all "whiskers" and the cordage is ready for use.

A three-strand rope, similar to manila rope may be made in the same manner as the two strand cordage, using three rolled strands tied together at one end with each strand being rolled in one direction and the three twisted together in the opposite direction to form the rope.

STRAW CRAFTS

Crafts using straw, have been used in Sweden and the other Scandinavian countries for centuries, not only for making Christmas decorations, but also for toys, favors, hats, and personal decorations.

To be successful, crafts of straw must be very carefully done.

For straw crafts, wheat straw is best, though other straw may be used.

It should be gathered carefully before harvesting, after the grain is ripe. Let the straw dry and handle it carefully to prevent bending and crushing. Dampen the straws before using them in craft projects.

A CHRISTMAS STAR

MATERIALS:

Straws matched for both size and color

Medium weight lashing cord or yarn, preferably red in
    color

Small sharp scissors

HOW TO MAKE:

Take seven straws of the same size and color and about 12
    inches long.

Tie them tightly in the center, keeping the straws side by
    side in a single plane.

Take seven more straws about 10 inches long, tying them
    tightly in the center, again remembering to keep them
    in a single plane, not in a round bunch. Tie them again,
    half way between the center and each end.

Do the same with seven more straws about 10 inches long.

Illustration showing the tying of the first set of straws for a Christmas Star. The completed and trimmed Christmas Star made of wheat straw.

Taking the first set of straws, tie them again one third of the way from the center to one end. Place both second and third sets of straws across the first set at this point and bind them tightly together. Tie the first set of straws again, one half of the way between the inserted straws and the end.

The tying is now completed.

Fan or bend the straws outward at the points where they are tied so that they look somewhat like the rays of the sun, trimming them with scissors to give them the shape shown in the illustration.

STRAW TINSEL

Using many short lengths of straw, three or four inches long, tie bunches of 5 or 6 straws in the center, fanning or bending them outwards. Then tie the bunches to lengths of colored yarn or cord with the bunches about 6 inches apart. Use these for decorating the Christmas Tree.

A STRAW BASKET

A beautiful straw basket may be made from straw sewn together with either colored cord, yarn, or raffia, and a darning needle.

MATERIALS:

Wheat straw gathered before harvesting, clean, and uncrushed or bent.

Colored cord, yarn, or raffia

A darning needle with a large eye

HOW TO MAKE:

Soak straws in water.

Starting with the smaller end of a dampened straw, sew it in a spiral. Use a figure-eight stitch, sewing over the top straw from the outside and under from the inside, and then under the next straw below from the inside, and over the same straw from the outside.

When the end of a straw is reached, insert the smaller end of a new straw into the larger end of the one being used.

When a flat mat the desired size of the bottom of the basket has been sewn, sew straws on top of the outer ring of straw, until the wall or side of the basket is a high as is desired.

A cover may be made in the same manner as the basket, but it must be one or two straw rings larger so as to fit over the bottom part of the basket.

A straw ring, sewn with a buttonhole stitch may be attached for a handle.

DRIED APPLE DOLLS

Dried apples, a few pieces of wire, and some rags, have been the makings of many, many dolls. The heads made from dried apples have a charm of their own for they have very wrinkled features indicating great age, something not normally seen in dolls. And they are not difficult to make.

MATERIALS:

Apple

Paring Knife

Medium weight wire for
    modeling arms, legs,
    and body

Rags for wrapping the wire
    framework

Watercolors for the face

Small beads for the eyes

Common pins to attach
    the eyes

Scraps of cloth for costumes

Yarn or cornsilk for hair

Glue or household cement

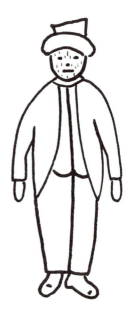

HOW TO MAKE:

Using a medium sized apple, pare the skin. Sculpture the
    head roughly showing the outlines of the eyes, nose, and
    mouth. Place the apple in a warm place where it can
    dry thoroughly. This may take several days.

After the apple is well dried, beads may be added for the eyes,
    using common pins to hold them in place. Watercolors
    may be used to give color to the features, especially,
    the lips, cheeks, and eyebrows.

Twist the wire into a rough body outline with body, arms,
    and legs. Leave enough wire at the neck to be pushed
    upwards through the dried apple head, bending the wires
    at the top of the head to hold it in place.

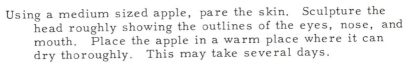

Wrap the wire framework with rags to give the body, legs, and arms the proper proportions. Tie or sew the rags in place.

Using scraps of cloth, dress the dolls in costumes of various countries or periods.

Add a peasant head-dress, sunbonnet, or hat, made from scraps of cloth or felt.

MUSICAL INSTRUMENTS

WHISTLES

Homemade whistles are a joy to make and are among the simpler of the musical instruments that can be made by almost anyone. There are many variations among whistles. Here are two of the easier ones to make.

A TWIG WHISTLE

MATERIALS:

Any small smooth-barked twig that peels easily in the spring or early summer will do the job. Willow and Moosefoot (Striped) Maple are among the best.

A sharp knife

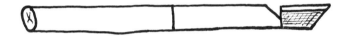

HOW TO MAKE:

Cut a twig, 6 - 7 inches long and about the size of a lead pencil. A twig without knots is best.

With a sharp knife cut one end of the twig on a slant, then cut around the twig and just through the bark from 2 -4 inches from that end.

Lay the twig on a solid surface, and with the handle of the knife tap the twig lightly until the bark between the cut and the slanted end is loosened and can be slipped from the twig.

Replace the bark on the twig.

About 3/4 inch from the slanted end, cut a V shaped hole in the bark and into the twig, cutting about 1/3 of the way through the twig (See illustration)

Remove the bark and cut off the end of the twig at the V-shaped cut.

From the top of this small end which you have cut off, trim a flat spot so that air can be blown through the whistle (See above illustration). Then replace this piece in the whistle.

This whistle should give a shrill piercing note when blown. The pitch can be changed by sliding the twig in and out of the end of the whistle as you blow.

A STICK WHISTLE

Any short piece of branch, green or dry, about 1 inch in diameter and about 6 inches long will make a whistle.

MATERIALS:

Piece of wood 1" X 6"

Jack-knife

1/2 inch drill or bit

HOW TO MAKE:

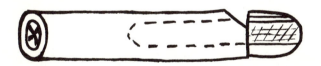

Broken lines show area of hole bored in stick whistle.

Using the drill or bit, bore a hole about 3 inches deep into one end of the piece of wood. Cut a V-shaped hole about 1/3 of the way through the wood about 3/4 inch from the end in which the hole has been drilled.

Cut a plug 3/4 inch long, trimming a flat place on the top for air to be blown through the whistle. Insert the plug with the flat side at the V shaped cut and blow. If the whistle does not blow well, trim a little more from the flat area of the plug. This will also change the tone slightly.

PIPES OF PAN

Few musical instruments are simple enough for boys and girls to make for themselves. One of special interest, however, is called the "Pipes of Pan". These are simple wind instruments made of hollow reeds, tubes, canes, or pipes, arranged together in a sequence of tones. They take their name from the ancient Greek God "Pan" who piped a tune on reeds taken from the river bank. Ancient shepherds also played on these primitive instruments.

USES:

These "Pipes of Pan" are useful in teaching chords; with a simple set of three pipes chording in the key of G, and to which additional notes may be added. The pipes may also be used to accompany voices or instruments.

MATERIALS:

Lengths of cane, bamboo, reeds, or other hollow tubes which can be closed at one end, or which have a natural closing such as the joints of bamboo.

Binding material such as raffia, basswood cordage, or twine.

HOW TO MAKE:

The note played is determined by the length of the hollow tube, measured from the open end to the point where the tube is closed.

To chord in the key of G, we need the notes D, G, and C.

The D reed or tube needs to be approximately 5 7/8 inches long from the open end to the closed part of the tube; the G reed 4 1/4 inches long; and the C reed 6 3/8 inches long (See illustration)

Cut the reeds a little too long so that the note can be corrected by trimming the reeds with a sharp knife, and testing with the correct notes on a piano.

The reeds can be fastened to cross-pieces by lashing with some type of binding material as listed above.

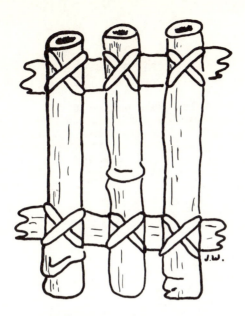

Finished pipes are lashed to cross pieces.

A COMPLETE SCALE

To make a complete scale in the key of C will require 8
    reeds, arranged in the following order and of the listed
    lengths.

C - 6 3/4 inches   D - 5 7/8 inches   E - 5 1/8 inches
F - 4 3/4 inches   G - 4 1/4 inches   A - 4 inches
B - 4 1/8 inches   C - 3 15/16 inches

To chord in 6 keys, use the following arrangement:

E - 5 1/8 inches   A - 4 1/8 inches   D - 5 7/8 inches
G - 4 1/4 inches   C - 6 3/4 inches   F - 5 inches
B^b - 7 inches E^b - 5 3/4 inches

Key of D is blown on pipes A, D, G.

Key of C on pipes G, C, F

Key of B flat on pipes F, B^b, E^b

Key of A on pipes E, A, D

Key of G on pipes D, G, C

Key of F on pipes C, F, B^b

SHEPHERDS PIPE

The ancient shepherds played pipes of their own making; made from a hollow reed or pieces of bamboo. They are rather easily made and can be played without ever having studied music. Legends tell us that the shepherds used these, not only for their own entertainment, but also to help quiet their sheep at night.

MATERIALS:

A piece of bamboo about 12 inches long and about 1 inch thick.

A cork or plug that will fit tightly into one end of the bamboo

A good sharp knife

A coping saw

A 3/16 inch drill

A small round file

HOW TO MAKE:

Clean the inside of the bamboo with file wire, or knife, carefully removing all inner partitions at the joints of the bamboo.

Measure 1/2 inch from one end, and carefully saw half way through (See illustration)

Saw mouthpiece into shape (See illustration)

One inch from the end of the mouthpiece, cut a hole in the top of

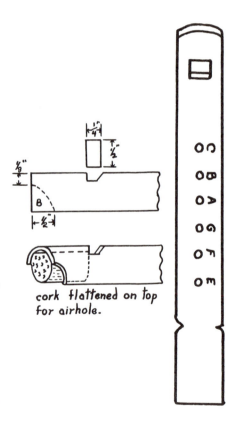

cork flattened on top for airhole.

Illustrations show where bamboo is trimmed and cut; the location of the flattened cork; and the positioning of the holes along the top of the pipe.

the bamboo. Make this hole 1/4 inch along the top of the bamboo, and 1/2 inch wide. Slant the edge farthest from the mouthpiece, giving it a sharp edge (See illustration)

Flatten one edge of the cork to allow for air passage, and fit the cork into the mouthpiece with the air passage at the top. The end of the cork should just reach the edge of the hole cut in the top of the bamboo.

Trim the end of the cork to match the shape of the mouthpiece.

TUNING THE PIPE:

Blow gently into the pipe. You will get the lowest possible note for the size of your pipe. This note can be used "as is", or it can be tuned to D in the piano by shortening the pipe a little at a time until the proper note is reached. Cut off from 1/8 to 1/4 inch at a time to raise the pitch.

Drill a 3/16 inch hole through the top of the pipe, one fourth of the length of the pipe, measuring from the end away from the mouthpiece. Sound this note. It should be the next note on the piano, or very close to it. To raise the note slightly, file the hole a little larger on the side nearest the mouthpiece. To lower it, file on the side away from the mouthpiece, filling in part of the original hole with plastic wood or wood-putty. Be sure that this note is the correct pitch before making the next hole.

Drill the second hole 7/8 inch nearer the mouthpiece. Tune as before to E of the piano.

Continue drilling holes and tuning to the next note of the piano until there are six holes, each one about 1/16 inch closer to the note or hole before it. Tune each note as you go along.

The last hole is made on the underside of the bamboo, directly beneath the hole nearest the mouthpiece. This will give a D, one octave higher than the original D.

This completes the making of the Shepherds' Pipe.

HOW TO PLAY:

Holding the pipe in both hands, place the left thumb over the hole on the under side of the pipe, and the first three fingers of the left hand over the three holes nearest the mouthpiece. The first three fingers of the right hand are placed over the remaining three holes.

The scale is played by starting with all holes covered. Removing the fingers one at a time, starting at the end away from the mouthpiece, will give the scale starting with D.

At the end of the first scale, the left thumb is removed from the hole on the underside, and the fingers replaced over the holes on the top for the start of the next octave higher. Removing the fingers one at a time as before, plays the next octave.

The notes that you now have on your pipe are D E F G A B C D E F G A B C

If you number the holes, starting with No. 1 on the underside; No. 2 the hole nearest the mouthpiece; No. 3 the next hole to No. 2 and so on, you can quickly write your own musc by numbers, or you may play by note with a little practice.

Try this on your pipe:

4 4 3 5 4 3

2 2 1 2 3 4

3 4 5 4

What tune is it?

Making a corn husk doll at the New York State Leader Training Camp. Also shown are a basswood bark birdhouse; glass paper weights; a leaf block print on a coaster; a necklace made of lacquered apricot pits; and block printed Christmas cards.

CORN-HUSK CRAFTS

Corn-husk dolls and animals were playthings for Indian children and were quickly adopted by the children of the early settlers. The husks were used for making other things, too. In the museum located in the Educational Building in Albany, N. Y., there is an interesting exhibit of Indian corn-husk crafts including mats, handbags, baskets, slippers, masks, and other articles

The best corn-husks for craft work are those from the inner layer of husks, next to the kernels of the corn. These are softer than the outside layers of husks. Dry the husks in the shade for a soft green color; or in the sun for a bleached white husk. The husks are readily dyed with any fabric dye, or with homemade dyes made from herbs, nuts, roots, and leaves of various kinds as suggested elsewhere in this publication.

CORN—HUSK DOLLS

MATERIALS:

Corn-husks

Corn silk for doll hair or animal manes

Needle and heavy thread

Glue or household cement

Colored yarns

Knife or shears

Pan of water

Paint and brush or pen and ink for making features

HOW TO MAKE:

Soften a number of husks in water.

Fold a large husk in half, inserting a wad of husks in the fold to round out the shape of the head. Wind heavy thread tightly around the base of the head, tying to make the neck. To form the arms, place a piece of twisted husk through the body just below the neck. Tie around the body below the arms to hold them in place, and tie about 1/4 inch from the ends of the arms, making the wrists and hands. Additional husks may be put in place for skirts or trousers and tied at the waist. Cut the bottom of the skirt straight across and the doll will stand by itself.

Boy dolls are made in the same way with legs made by slitting the skirt up the center, and then tying at the ankles to form trousers and feet.

Coats or shawls are made by placing pieces of husk criss-cross over the shoulders and tying at the waist. Hats, aprons, etc., may be made of husks and glued or cemented in place. Dyed husks make colorful clothes.

Hair, eyebrows, moustaches, etc., may be made of cornsilk or yarn and glued or cemented in place. Eyes, nose, and mouth may be added with water-colors or pen and ink.

CORN—HUSK HOT PADS

Corn husks have an excellent value as insulation; are easily woven; and so are fine for making hot-pads for the table.

MATERIALS:

Corn husks

Needle and thread

A hot pad, small basket, and small mat made of corn husks.

HOW TO MAKE:

Tear husks into narrow strips. Using three strips, tied
together at one end, tack the tied end to a board and
start braiding the strips. Add new strips of husks as
the ends are reached, making sure to stagger the ends
as pieces are added, so that the braid will not pull apart.

Or: Husks may be tied together making long strips or strands
about the size of a lead pencil and then wrapped spirally
with wet husks about 1/2 inch in width.

Either of the above type of strands may be coiled in a spiral
fashion and sewed together with needle and thread to
make hot pads of any size.

CIRCULAR LOOM WOVEN HOT PADS

MATERIALS:

Circular piece of medium-weight cardboard 6 - 8 inches in
diameter

Heavy twine, carpet warp, or heavy yarn

Corn husks

Large darning needle

HOW TO MAKE:

Punch a small hole in the center of the cardboard disk

Cut notches, about 1/4 inch deep, and about 1/2 inch apart
Around the edge of the cardboard disk. Space these so
that there is an uneven number of notches.

Tie a knot in one end of the thread, yarn, or cord being
used. Slip this knot into one of the notches, bring the
thread up through the notch, to the center of the disk,
and down through the hole in the center. Go across the
back of the disk and up through the next notch, across
the top and down through the center hole. Continue this
until the loom is completely threaded. Tie the end of
the thread to the knot where you started at the first notch.

Tear the wet cornhusks into narrow strips and thread one of
these into the darning needle. Beginning at the center
of the cardboard loom, weave around the center, going
first over and then under the warp threads. Make certain that each row is on the opposite side of the warp
thread, than the preceding row.

When adding a new strip of husk, go back two or three warp
threads from the end of the last strip, weaving over and
under the same warp threads. Pull the strips tightly
together. When one side of the loom has been filled,
turn the loom over and fill the other side.

If any cardboard shows when the loom has been filled, carefully trim it with shears, filling in the spaces with
weaving. The cardboard disk is left inside the mat.

Add a fringe to the mat by looping doubled strips of husk
through the last strip of weaving, pulling the ends
through the loop and trimming with shears.

CORN—HUSK BASKETS, SLIPPERS, HAND—BAGS, ETC.

Corn-husks are braided as directed in the above article on
Corn-Husk Hot Pads.

HOW TO MAKE:

Baskets are made by taking strands of braided corn-husks
and sewing them together. Make a spiral row of strands
for the bottom, and sewing strands on top of each other
for the sides of the basket. A top may be made in the
same manner. Handles, made from braided husks, may
be sewn to the sides of the basket.

Slippers are made similarly, sewing braided corn-husks
together to form the sole of the slipper, and then sewing
up the sides as in the making of baskets.

To make a handbag, sew braided strips together to make a
large flat mat; double the mat, sewing the edges together,
and attach a braided handle.

CORN—HUSK MAT

Corn-husk mats were probably first made by the Indians,
but Great Grandmother was quick to adapt them to the log-
cabin of the frontier. They had many uses. They were
sometimes used for sleeping mats; sometimes on the floor.
Today they can serve the same purpose as the cocoa fiber
mats used at the door to wipe mud from the shoes.

MATERIALS:

Corn-husks

Medium weight cord

Pieces of burlap, hemmed to the size of the mat desired

Needle and heavy thread

HOW TO MAKE:

Tie together two pieces of cord a few inches longer than the
length of the burlap backing. Fasten one end of the cords
to a nail at a height convenient for working.

Using corn-husks about 3/4 inch wide, tie "Egyptian Knots"
the entire length of the cords, forming a strip of corn-
husk knots the length of the mat to be made. Several
strips of these knotted husks are sewn side by side to the
burlap backing to form the mat. As each strip is attached, trim the knotted husks evenly to about one inch
in length, with shears. When dry this will make a very
durable mat.

The "Egyptian Knot" is tied in the following manner: (See
illustration, p. 79)

Lay a strip of husk across the top of the two cords, pulling
the ends of the husk up through the center between the
cords. Pull each knot tight as it is made, and pull it
tightly against the previous knot tied.

A CORN—HUSK BROOM

The stiff outer layers of corn-husks make excellent brooms for the fireplace. Save the outside husks for these while using the softer inner husks for other crafts.

MATERIALS:

Outer corn-husks

Dowel or piece of wood 10 - 18 inches long and about 3/4 inch diameter

Strong cord

Tying the Egyptian Knot.

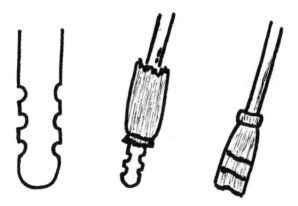

Illustrations show how notches are cut in the broom handle; how the tiers of husks are laid and tied extending up the handle; and how they are finally turned downward and tied to complete the broom.

HOW TO MAKE:

Cut three sets of notches 3/4 inch apart and 1/8 inch deep,
  on opposite sides of one end of the stick selected for the
  broom handle, with the first notch 1 1/2 inches from
  the end.

Lay moistened corn-husks lengthways of the handle with the
  ends across the innermost notch, and the long ends of the
  husks extending up the handle. Bind them tightly at the
  notch with cord.

Do the same at the other two notches, each time with the
  long ends of the husks extending up the handle.

Now, turn each tier of husks downwards, starting with the
  tier nearest the end of the broom. Bind them tightly
  before turning down the next tier.

Trim the husks if needed, and the broom is finished.

WITCH-HAZEL BROOMS

In colonial days, witch-hazel brooms were standard equipment in the home. Large brooms were made to sweep the floors and smaller ones hung at the end of the fireplace to sweep the hearth. Very small, stubby brooms took the place of our present-day choreboys and pot-cleaners for scrubbing pots and pans.

USES:

Witch-hazel brooms are easy to make in a variety of sizes, and can be used at home, or will make very satisfactory gifts to those with a modern fireplace and hearth.

MATERIALS:

Jackknife with a short, sharp-pointed blade

Stick of witch-hazel wood, preferably without knots; at least 1 1/2 inches in diameter and about 2 feet long. Larger pieces make larger brooms. (The witch-hazel should be cut fresh, and should be used before it dries).

Heavy cord, raffia, or other binding material

HOW TO MAKE:

Mark the center of the stick, measuring from each end.

At points about 1/2 inch from this center, cut through the bark around the stick.

Peel the bark from one end of the stick to the point where it has been cut through

At the peeled end, using the point of the knife blade, pick out small splinters, tearing them down the stick until they break loose. Do this in a uniform pattern around the end of the stick. Each time around the stick, the splinters will become longer until they peel all the way to where the bark remains on the stick. Leave these attached to the stick as they will form the splints of the broom. Peel and pull back these long splinters until the entire end of the stick has been peeled away. (The knife is used only to start the splinters by picking them out

WITCH—HAZEL BROOMS

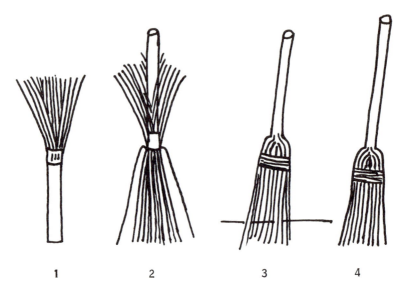

1   2   3   4

Drawings show the four major steps in the making of a witch-hazel broom.

Photo shows the partially constructed and the completed and carved fireplace
broom made of witch-hazel.

from the end of the stick. The finer the splinters are, the better the broom being made. They are pulled down by hand, and <u>not</u> shaved down with the knife.)

Cut out the short stub remaining and tie a string around the loose splints to hold them together while working on the other end of the stick.

Now peel the bark from the other end to the point where it was cut through, leaving the one inch ring of bark remaining in the center. Pick out and pull splinters from this end in the same fashion until a layer at least two splinters thick remains attached all of the way around the broom. Turn these downwards over the main part of the broom and tie around the broom near the ends to hold the splinters in place.

Bind the broom tightly, just below the handle with heavy cord, raffia, or other binding material.

Trim the broom splints evenly with a sharp hatchet on a wooden block.

The handle may be scraped smooth or carved to please the maker, and the splints may be dyed if desired. Drill a small hole at the end of the handle and attach a thong for hanging the broom.

SNAKESKINS

SKINS AND VERTEBRAE

Occasionally large snakes are killed in the vicinity of camp or on the roadway. Don't go hunting snakes for their skins and bones, but if one should be found dead, add to the interest of the nature program with one of these projects.

USES:

Belts

Trophies

Hatbands

Nature Collections

MATERIALS:

Salt

Hot water

Commercial sulphuric acid

Washing soda

Board for drying

Crock or earthenware jar

HOW TO MAKE:

Skin the snake by slitting the underside from head to tail and peeling off the skin.

Remove any flesh by scraping with a dull blade.

Prepare a salt solution of 1 pint of salt to two quarts of hot water.

When this cools, add slowly one-half ounce of commercial sulphuric acid.

Soak the skin in this solution for one week.

Wash thoroughly in water, then soak for one hour in five quarts of water to which has been added one half cup of common washing soda. Rinse well. Tack on a board and dry in the shade.

A belt may be made by cutting the skin to the desired length and width; attaching a buckle to one end, and trimming and punching the other end. A better belt is made by folding the edges in and cementing or sewing along the edges; or by cementing the snakeskin to a plain leather backing. (Save the bones of the snake for other nature crafts. The individual vertebrae are useful in costume jewelry, and may closely resemble miniature steer skulls. They may be cleaned and bleached by boiling and letting stand in a solution of household bleach; or in ammonia or hydrogen peroxide. Use them on earrings, tie-clasps, pins, and neckerchief slides.)

FIRES AND FLAMES

COLORED FLAMES

Pine cones and other native materials may be treated with a variety of chemicals to produce colored flames that add a special attraction to the fireplace or the campfire. A bag of these treated materials makes an excellent gift to a friend who has a fireplace.

MATERIALS:

Cones - clean and dry

Other native materials such as driftwood; knots; goldenrod galls; etc.

Chemicals - commercial forms available from local drug-store or farm supply store. These will produce color as follows:

Red	- Strontium chloride
Green	- Barium chloride
Bluish green	- Copper sulphate
Orange	- Calcium chloride
Lavender	- Potassium chloride
Yellow	- Sodium chloride (common salt)

(Sodium and calcium colors will hide those of other metals)

IMPORTANT - Nitrates and Chlorates are very inflammable. Do not use them.

HOW TO MAKE:

Dissolve each chemical to be used in a separate container (a wooden container is suggested) - one pound of chemical to one gallon of water.

Soak the cones or other materials in the solution for a few minutes to several hours. Drain and dry. Large numbers of cones may be dipped in a mesh or burlap bag and hung up to drain and dry.

Another method is to dip the cones in a thin solution of glue
and water and dust them with the powdered chemicals
while the glue is still tacky.

CHEMICAL FIRE STARTERS

Chemical fire starters do not actually belong in a book of
nature crafts, but are being included here for their interest
to campers and craft personnel. Campers are awed by
campfires that seem to start of their own accord, or at a
signal of some kind from the camp director or the Indian
Chief presiding at the campfire. Two methods of lighting
the campfire by chemical means are described here.

SULPHURIC ACID, POTASSIUM CHLORATE, & SUGAR

Sulphuric acid and potassium chlorate are dangerous and
should be used only by a responsible person. The acid
should be kept stored in a bottle where there is little danger
of breakage. In case the acid is accidently spilled on clothing or skin, it should be <u>immediately</u> diluted with water,
and quickly washed with water and soda before it can eat into
the material or burn the flesh.

MATERIALS:

Commercial sulphuric acid (from drug store)

Potassium Chlorate   "   "   "

Sugar

2 waxed paper cups

Thread or string

Small cardboard box - about 5 X 10 inches by 2 inches deep.

HOW TO USE:

Build a log-cabin firelay

Poke a small twig or stick through holes near the center of
the cardboard box, so the stick goes crossways of the
box, parallel to and about 1 1/2 inch from the bottom
of the box.

Nest two paper cups together, and tie a thread to the lip of
one. Set the cups in the box and run the thread through

88

a small hole in the opposite end of the box so that a pull
on the thread will cause the paper cups to upset over the
cross-stick. (The nested paper cups are for added protection from the acid.)

Mix equal parts of potassium chlorate and sugar (2 - 3 tea-
spoonfuls of each) and pour this mixture into the box in
the end opposite the paper cups.

Pour about 1/4 cup of sulphuric acid into the paper cup.
When this is upset and makes contact with the potassium
chlorate and sugar mixture, the fire will start.

After pouring the acid into the cup, arrange fine kindling
around and above the cardboard box in such a way that
it will not prevent the paper cup being upset when the
thread is pulled. (A stone placed in the bottom of the
cup may add to its stability.)

The thread may be hidden by running it beneath small sticks
or stones to a point some distance from the firelay. A
careful pull on the thread at the desired time during a
prayer to the "Great Spirit" to send fire, will cause the
fire to start going in dramatic fashion with a great
amount of intense crackling and smoke.

POTASSIUM PERMANGANATE & GLYCERINE

These materials are perfectly safe to handle and store.
Fresh materials work best, however, and older chemicals
should be tried out in advance of using to make sure they
work effectively.

The time of reaction between these two chemicals is not
easily controlled, but fire will usually start in about two
minutes after the chemicals are brought into contact with
each other.

MATERIALS:

Potassium permanganate (from drugstore)

Glycerine

Paper cup (preferably cone-shaped)

HOW TO USE:

Build a fire-lay of any type

About two minutes before the fire is to be started, place in
the base of the firelay among the kindling, a paper cup
containing about one teaspoonful of potassium permanganate, saturated with 6 - 8 drops of glycerine. Chemical action will set the paper cup on fire in about two
minutes.

PLASTER CASTING

Plaster casts are one of the best ways of preserving copies or records of animal tracks, fossils, etc., and may also be used for mounting collections of rocks and minerals, fossils, small skulls, bones, etc., or for making leaf prints, prints of flowers, and mounts for cones and other materials.

USES:

Plaster casts provide a way of making a collection of animal tracks; for preserving and identifying a variety of collections; for decorative use as mounted wall plaques; in making nature - motif book-ends; and a variety of other ideas.

MATERIALS:

Plaster of Paris

Clean water

Stick for stirring

Container for mixing (a plastic mixing bowl is excellent for it is easily cleaned when the plaster has dried in it)

Strips of tin or cardboard about 2 inches wide to hold plaster in place when casting animal tracks, or when mounting various items.

HOW TO MAKE:

The best animal tracks for plaster casting, are those tracks found singly, with clear and distinct prints in sand or mud. Look for them along streams, particularly where mud or fine sand has been washed along the edges of small pools.

When the track has been selected, make a round or oblong form of the tin or cardboard strips. The form should be 2 - 3 inches wider than the print to be cast. Push this form down into the mud or sand, leaving about one inch projecting above the surface, and being careful not to disturb the track.

Mix the plaster of Paris and water, stirring it with a stick, to a thick, soupy consistency. Pour this plaster into the track, filling the form to about one inch in depth. Leave this in place for 2 - 3 hours to harden, being certain to mark the spot well so that you can find the cast on your return.

Wash out the mixing dish and the stick for stirring if you plan to do more casts. The next batch of plaster will not harden satisfactorily if it is mixed in a container in which partially hardened plaster remains.

When the cast has hardened, remove it from the mud or sand, remove the form, and wash the print well in running water. You will find that you have a very nice negative of the original track if you have been careful with your casting.

Similar casts can be made of fossils, coating the fossils first with vaseline or light oil to keep the plaster from sticking permanently. The strips for forms, need not be used on small fossils, where only a teaspoonful or so of plaster is needed.

Collections of rocks, minerals, fossils, animal bones, skulls, cones, etc., may be mounted by casting a plaque in a tin or cardboard form on a smooth background, and inserting the pieces of the collection into the plaster while it is still in a liquid state.

Bookends may be cast by building an outline from modeling clay, and casting the plaster in this form. Collections of rocks, minerals, cones, and other materials, may be incorporated in the bookends for decoration while the plaster is still liquid.

Try making casts of leaves and flowers, laying the leaf or flower on a smooth dish and pouring the wet plaster over it. These may be painted when dry. It is also possible to pour the plaster into a form, and then press the leaf or flower into the plaster, leaving the imprint when the plaster has dried.

TERRARIUMS

A terrarium is a small garden, field, or woodland scene
enclosed in glass. It holds soil and growing plants, and may
serve as a home for insects and small animals. It can be
a miniature landscape representing a variety of scenes and
seasons.

USES:

A terrarium may be a decoration, or it may serve as a place
   to observe and study nature.

MATERIALS:

Terrariums may be of any size. They may be made of glass
   jars standing vertically or lying on their sides. If on
   its side, a wooden cradle or a piece of modeling clay
   will prevent rolling.

A terrarium should have a cover to prevent the evaporation
   of water, and the escape of insects or other wildlife,
   but one which can be raised to allow moisture to escape
   if there is too much present. Excess moisture is indi-
   cated by mildew, and by wet sides and top of the terrarium.

For a rectangular terrarium we need:

   6 panes of glass of any convenient size, preferably single
   thickness.

   1 or more rolls of 1" or 1 1/2" waterproof adhesive
   tape (amount needed depends on the size of the terrarium
   being made.

   A sheet metal base made of galvanized material or
   aluminum is convenient, especially if the terrarium is
   to be in use over a long period of time and may be sub-
   jected to considerable handling.

HOW TO MAKE:

Tape four pieces of glass according to the following diagram;
   leaving a space between each piece the thickness of a
   pane of glass so that the assembled pieces may be folded
   into box shape. Stand the four pieces on edge and tape
   the remaining corner to form a bottomless box.

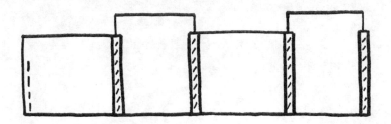

This illustration shows the positioning of panes of glass
as they are being taped together to make a terrarium.

Turn this box upside down and tape on the fifth pane for the
bottom.

Now carefully tape the inside of each joint to give the terrarium strength. Do this by attaching the tape evenly along
one side of the joint, working the tape into the joint and
onto the other side.

Tape the sixth pane of glass to the top, forming a hinge at
the back of the terrarium, leaving the other three edges
free to be opened like a trap-door.

Cover all raw edges of glass for protection, and add a tab
to the front of the cover for easy opening.

FILLING THE TERRARIUM:

Decide on the habitat to be shown, such as a field, woodland,
bog, stream edge, desert, garden, etc.

Place about an inch of coarse clean gravel in the bottom of
the terrarium, then on a field trip collect materials
representative of the habitat selected.

Collect soil from the chosen habitat.

Suggested materials to collect are small plants; suitable
small animals if they are to be included; interesting
pieces of wood, mossy stones, rocks, lichens, mosses,
fungi, dead leaves, acorns, shells, etc.

In filling the terrarium, put an inch or more of the habitat
soil over the gravel, adding a few pieces of charcoal to
absorb odors, then add the collected materials one at
a time, making a natural habitat scene. Place the larger

94

Terrariums being filled at the New York State Leader Training Camp. Note the terrarium made of part of a coffee-maker, and covered with a plastic to retard evaporation of water.

plants at the back and the smaller ones near the front of the terrarium, but don't overcrowd. Leave room for the plants to grow. Spread the roots carefully, covering them well with soil or humus. When finished sprinkle the soil until it is moist but not wet. Usually no more moisture will need be added for 1 - 2 months. The cover of the terrarium is normally kept closed to maintain a suitable humidity, but it may be raised occasionally for a change of air, or to allow excess moisture to escape. Mold or mildew may develop if the terrarium is too warm and humid.

Ponds or lakes may be made in the terrarium, of small inconspicuous dishes, sunk to their rims and edged with

moss or grasses.   Make the lake bottom of a thin layer
of fine sand.   Keep the water clean.

Useful in woodland terrariums are small ferns, mosses,
partridge-berry, small violets, hepaticas, tree seedlings,
lichens, fungi, snail shells, pieces of bark, acorns,
nuts, brown leaves, a rock for a ledge near a pool, etc.

Desert terrariums need plenty of clean sand with small cacti
set in tiny pots and hidden in the sand.

Small animals such as tiny turtles, toads, frogs, salaman-
ders, newts, and snakes add interest to a terrarium but
need to be fed.   All animals need a hiding place, perhaps
made of a branch, stone, or piece of wood.   Insects may
provide needed food.   Snakes and turtles need considerable sunshine.

THINGS TO NOTICE:

In your terrarium you may be able to see the differences in
plants and their ways of growing; the life histories of
insects and animals; the relationship of living things to
moisture, heat, light, and air.

You may wish to label the materials used, with tiny guideposts inside the terrarium; or draw a chart of the terrarium calling attention to the items of interest.

A terrarium is a fine place to lay out a miniature nature
trail.

COLLECTING SPIDER-WEBS

Spider-webs are amazing creations with the spider as an engineer whose feats rank even above those of the human engineer.

Collecting spider-webs takes little skill or equipment, and gives a real thrill.

USES:

Collections of spider-webs may be mounted in a notebook and identified by the variety of spider making the web. They can be framed as wall decorations and used beneath the glass on a tray or coffee table.

MATERIALS:

Dark colored construction paper

Spray can of white paint or enamel

Scissors

Turpentine

Old newspapers

Rags or paper towels for removing turpentine.

HOW TO MAKE:

Spiders spin their webs across open spaces where they may catch insects. Guy lines act as supports for the wheel-shaped webs.

Find a suitable web on a quiet day.

Spread newspapers behind the web to catch the waste part of the spray paint. If there is a spider on the web, urge him off with a piece of grass. Spray the web lightly with paint on both sides, using short bursts of spray, and spray with any breeze that may be present.

When all threads are lightly coated with paint, place a piece of construction paper beneath the web, bringing it carefully against the whole web, holding it steady.

Cut the guy lines at the edge of the construction paper, and
allow the painted web to dry.

Clean up with turpentine and paper towels.

INSECT CAGES

A glass jar or a glass box, similar to a terrarium but covered with screening, makes a good cage for keeping and
raising insects.

The bottom of the cage may consist of soil containing growing
plants serving for food, cover, and a resting place for insects.
2 - 3 inches of moist soil provides a place for grasshoppers
and crickets to lay their eggs; for some kinds of caterpillars
to pupate; and for ants and other types of burrowers to make
their homes.

Small bottles of water may be buried in the soil also, in
which plants and vines are placed to keep them fresh to provide food and cover for insects.

Leaf eaters should have fresh food, usually the kind on which
they are found. Crickets and grasshoppers like fine bread
crumbs, tiny pieces of fruit, grass and fresh plants. Spiders
need live flies and other insects. Spiders that spin webs
need a tall plant or piece of small brush for their webs.

MATERIALS:

Glass jars or panes of glass

Waterproof tape if glass panes are used

Scrap wire screening

Tops of tin cans or can covers

Plaster of Paris

HOW TO MAKE:

Glass jars may have screening or cheesecloth tied over their
    tops

Glass cages may also be made similarly to terrariums but
    with wire screen tops.

A wire cage, especially suitable for caterpillars that pupate,
    is made from a roll of wire screening shaped into a
    cylinder of any convenient size to fit inside a can cover,
    and of any convenient height from 2 - 8 inches. Sew up
    the side of the cylinder with a heavy thread or a wire
    taken from the side of the screening.

Place the wire cylinder inside the can cover and add enough
   Plaster of Paris to hold the wire in place and to weight
   the end to hold the cage upright. Mix the plaster with
   water to a soupy consistency and pour it into the cover
   used for the base of the cage.

The top from a tin can makes an effective cover for the cage,
   or one can be made from screening.

AN INSECT ZOO

It is not necessary to have wild animals to make a zoo, for wild insects are just as interesting, and are available to anyone who has the desire to "bring them back alive", and then put them on exhibit, for an insect zoo can be easily be made, filled, and set up on a table-top.

USES:

An insect zoo can give many hours of pleasure, and can certainly provide an opportunity for studying the habits of a wide variety of remarkable living creatures.

MATERIALS:

Insect cages made of wire screening

Terrariums

Insect foods (to be collected)

Books for the identification of insects collected

HOW TO MAKE:

See the articles in this publication on the making of insect cages, terrariums, and insect-catching nets.

TIPS ON COLLECTING AND FEEDING:

Field Crickets - Place an inch or so of soil in the bottom of the cage. Small containers of water should also be sunk into the soil. For food, use small pieces of soaked bread, tiny pieces of lettuce, little dabs of peanut-butter and very small amounts of mashed potatoes.

Walking Sticks - Place a piece of sod in the bottom of the cage. Keep the grass growing by adding occasional water. The grass will serve as food, and a small dish of water should be added for drinking.

Grasshoppers - Same as for walking sticks.

Caterpillars - Leaves of the same plant on which they are found should be used for food until they enter the chrysalis or coocon stage. Keep them in the cage until they emerge as butterflies or moths.

Praying Mantis - These are a carnivorous insect. Feed them flies and other small insects or tiny pieces of meat. Once the egg-mass has been layed, keep this in your cage until the young emerge.

Click Beetles - These are also carnivorous. Feed them soft-bodied insects and meal worms. Keep a small container of water in the cage.

INSECT COLLECTING EQUIPMENT

INSECT COLLECTING NET

MATERIALS:

3-foot broom handle or one inch dowel.

5 feet heavy wire

Mosquito netting - 3 X 5 ft.

5 feet heavy cord or soft wire for wrapping handle

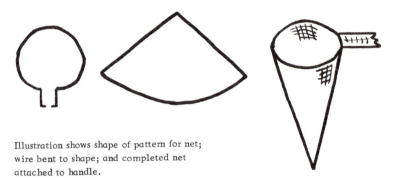

Illustration shows shape of pattern for net;
wire bent to shape; and completed net
attached to handle.

HOW TO MAKE:

Cut a paper pattern before cutting the net. The pattern
should roll into cone shape and be as deep as the netting
is wide (3 ft.)

Bend the heavy wire into shape as illustrated

Bore a hole through the end of the handle, and cut grooves in
the handle between the bored hole and the end and lengthways of the handle, to hold the wire frame tightly.

Cut netting into the shape of the pattern and sew it into cone
shape.

Hem the edge of the net and slide it over the wire frame.

Attach the wire frame to the handle with the bent ends of the
wire in the hole bored in the handle, and the wire lying
in the grooves cut in the handle.

Wire or bind securely in place.

USING THE NET:

Swing the net in wide sweeping motions. Insects need not
always be seen to be caught. Sweeping the net through
grass; among tree or shrub leaves; or near an electric
light at night; may be very productive.

WATER INSECTS:

A small hand or kitchen sieve is used to collect water insects.
Draw it through the water beneath overhanging banks,
or lift stones, and quickly sweep the sieve across the
bottom. Transfer all water insects caught to a jar of
the same water. There they can be studied and identified. Look carefully, for many water insects are tiny
and almost transparent. A magnifying glass may be
very helpful.

INSECT KILLING BOTTLE

MATERIALS:

Pint jar with lid and sealing ring or rubber.

Piece of heavy cardboard

Several thick rubber bands or scraps of innertube.

Small bottle of carbon tetrachloride (Chloroform or ethyl
acetate may be used. Do not use cyanide)

HOW TO MAKE:

Place scraps of rubber inside
jar.

Saturate rubber with carbon
tetrachloride (pour off
excess)

Cut cardboard disk to fit
tightly inside jar over the
rubber scraps.

Keep the jar sealed except
when putting in or re-
moving insects.

An ordinary jar with screw-top makes
an excellent insect killing jar.

The carbon tetrachloride will remain effective for about
one month. When necessary remove the cardboard disk
and add more carbon tetrachloride.

HOW TO USE:

Select the insects to be killed. Do not kill them indiscrimi-
nately, but only those which you wish for your collection or for future identification.

Remove the top, place the insect inside, and it is quickly
killed without suffering. Do not leave insects in the
jar for a long time, but as soon as feasible, remove
insects for mounting. Most insects are mounted with
their wings closed, but some such as butterflies and
moths are mounted with wings spread.

INSECT SPREADING BOARD

MATERIALS:

2 pieces of softwood - 1/4" X 2" X 12"

2 pieces of softwood - 1/2" X 2" X 4 1/2"

1 piece plywood - 1/4" X 4 1/2" X 12"

1 piece cork or balsa wood - 1/2" X 1" X 12"

Glue and small brads

Insect pins (common pins may be used)

HOW TO MAKE:

Glue and nail the 4 1/2" pieces on edge across the ends of
the plywood.

Glue and nail the 12" pieces of softwood across and between
the 4 1/2" pieces, leaving a 1/2" crack in the center
between these pieces.

Glue and nail the strip of cork or balsa to the underside of
the 12" slats of softwood, covering the crack between
the slats.

HOW TO USE:

Pin butterflies and moths as soon as possible after killing,
and before they are dry, inserting an insect pin through

the thorax (main part of the body), and then through the cork so that the body rests on the cork, in the crack between the slats of the spreading board.

With the point of another pin, move the wings forward so that they are well spread.

When the wings have been spread, place narrow strips of paper across each wing, from front to back. Fasten down with pins at the ends of the paper strips.

Leave the moths or butterflies until they are well dried, when they may be moved into a display box.

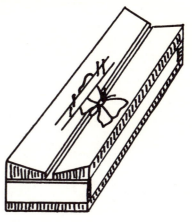

Illustration shows the construction of a spreading board, and the pinning of a butterfly or moth. Note that the pins do not go through the wings.

INSECT DISPLAY BOXES

MATERIALS:

1 piece glass 18 3/4" X 23 1/2" (a standard size)

2 pieces softwood 3/4" X 3 5/8" X 24"

1 piece softwood 3/4" X 3 5/8" X 18"

1 piece softwood 3/4" X 3" X 18"

1 piece 1/4" plywood 19 1/2" X 24"

1 piece 1/2" celotex 18" X 22 1/2"

Small brads and glue

HOW TO MAKE:

Draw a pencil line the length of each of the 2 pieces of soft-wood 24" long, 5/8" from one edge. Do the same to the piece 3/4" X 3 5/8" X 18". Saw a groove or slot on the outside of these lines. The pane of glass should be able to slide in this slot in the completed box, so it should be just slightly wider than the thickness of the glass.

Nail and glue together the parts
numbered 2, 3 and 4 in
the illustration. Attach
the plywood bottom, num-
ber 5. The celotex,
number 6, is fastened to
the bottom on the inside
of the box. The glass,
number 1, slides into
the slots on parts 2 and 4.

HOW TO USE:

No. 3 insect pins are preferred
though common pins may
be used.

Labels should be made and
placed on the pins with
the insects. They are
made from stiff paper,
1/2" X 1", and include
the name of the insect, name of the collector, and the
date and place where collected. They should be printed
with a very fine pen. Two labels are often used, placed
1/4" apart and 1/4" below the insect on the pin.

The numbers in the above diagram are
referred to in the text.

The mounting pins are pushed through the body of the insect,
usually at one side of the thorax, and the insect pushed
to within 1/4" of the head of the pin, with the labels
below. The point of the pin is then inserted in the celotex of the bottom of the display box.

Tiny insects such as aphids, flea beetles, etc., are attached
to the points of tiny triangles of paper with household
cement, and the pins stuck through the wider part of the
paper triangles, then labeled the same as above.

In beginning an insect collection, start with freshly killed
insects representing each of the five major groups of
insects, a bug, a beetle, a bee or fly, a grasshopper,
and a butterfly. Then add other groups as they are collected and identified.

There are many good books and pamphlets which will aid in
identifying the insects you collect. One of these is listed
in the bibliography at the end of this publication.

BIRD HOUSES AND FEEDERS

A family of bluebirds calls this home.

Bird houses made of native materials such as bark, hollow logs, slabwood, and such, are rustic and have a great appeal both to birds, and to home owners. In addition they are easy to make for they do not need a painted finish. Crudely made birdhouses often look better and draw birds quicker than those which require a lot of careful work.

There are those who would prefer to spend more time and build a more elaborate birdhouse, and such are also very acceptable if well designed.

The general idea of a bird house is to have a roof, floor, walls, and small room for the nest. Most people are apt to make the room too large.

HOME STYLES FOR BIRDS

Most important in getting the tenant you want, is having the correct size of house, inside depth, diameter of the entrance, and the distance of the birdhouse from the ground. Following is a simple reference table for the more common birds. (See page 109)

Metal guards around a tree or post prevent cats from climbing to nests or bird feeders.

BIRD FEEDERS

Bird foods may be scarce during late winter and early spring and at this time feeders are particularly welcome by birds.

Any piece of scrap board will make a feeding tray. Another piece will make a shield from the wind, and still another can be a roof. Leave feeders as open as possible. Use baby-chick grains, broken peanuts, canary seed, millet, bread crumbs, sunflower seeds, oatmeal, suet, peanut-butter, pieces of apple, and raisins.

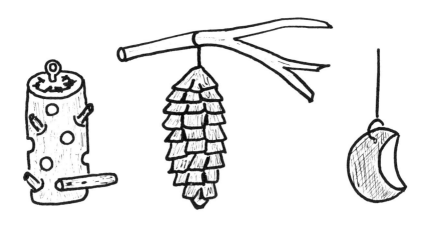

Simple bird feeders.

BIRDHOUSE REFERENCE TABLE

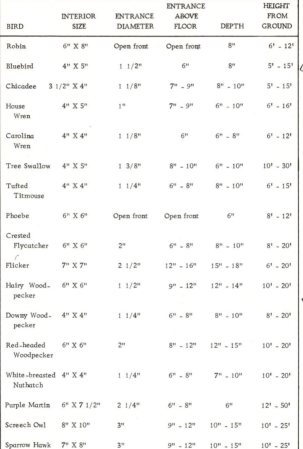

BIRD	INTERIOR SIZE	ENTRANCE DIAMETER	ENTRANCE ABOVE FLOOR	DEPTH	HEIGHT FROM GROUND
Robin	6" X 8"	Open front	Open front	8"	6' - 12'
Bluebird	4" X 5"	1 1/2"	6"	8"	5' - 15'
Chicadee	3 1/2" X 4"	1 1/8"	7" - 9"	8" - 10"	5' - 15'
House Wren	4" X 5"	1"	7" - 9"	6" - 10"	6' - 16'
Carolina Wren	4" X 4"	1 1/8"	6"	6" - 8"	6' - 12'
Tree Swallow	4" X 5"	1 3/8"	8" - 10"	6" - 10"	10' - 30'
Tufted Titmouse	4" X 4"	1 1/4"	6" - 8"	8" - 10"	6' - 15'
Phoebe	6" X 6"	Open front	Open front	6"	8' - 12'
Crested Flycatcher	6" X 6"	2"	6" - 8"	8" - 10"	8' - 20'
Flicker	7" X 7"	2 1/2"	12" - 16"	15" - 18"	6' - 20'
Hairy Wood-pecker	6" X 6"	1 1/2"	9" - 12"	12" - 14"	10' - 20'
Downy Wood-pecker	4" X 4"	1 1/4"	6" - 8"	8" - 10"	8' - 20'
Red-headed Woodpecker	6" X 6"	2"	8" - 12"	12" - 15"	10' - 20'
White-breasted Nuthatch	4" X 4"	1 1/4"	6" - 8"	7" - 10"	10' - 20'
Purple Martin	6" X 7 1/2"	2 1/4"	6" - 8"	6"	12' - 50'
Screech Owl	8" X 10"	3"	9" - 12"	10" - 15"	10' - 25'
Sparrow Hawk	7" X 8"	3"	9" - 12"	10" - 15"	10' - 25'

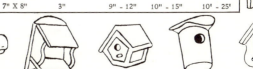

A mixture of peanut-butter and chopped raisins placed in holes bored in a small log, makes an excellent feeder. Add one or more perches as in the illustration. Hang with a screw-eye and wire 8 - 10 feet from the ground.

Pour a mixture of melted unsalted fat and birdseed over an open pine cone. When this has hardened, hang it from a limb of a tree.

Make a feeder from a coconut, cutting out a part of one side of the shell, leaving a lip to hold food inside, and filling occasionally with bird seed. Hang with a wire through holes bored in the top of the shell.

Make a suet feeder by simply tacking a piece of hardware cloth (large mesh screen) over a piece of suet on the trunk of a tree. Birds, especially woodpeckers, will come to this suet feeder.

Make a bird feeder from your discarded Christmas tree, decorating it with strings of popcorn (unsalted) and cranberries. Tie on a few dried ears of corn; orange rinds and nut shells stuffed with a mixture of peanut-butter and chopped raisins; and pieces of suet. Tie the tree to a post where the winds will not blow it down.

Keep a record of the birds that come to your feeder. You will soon get to know certain birds that are regular visitors. Study their personalities, for you will find that each bird has his own. Some are sedate and serious; some are naggers; some are selfish and others share their food; some seem to like to pick a fight. Soon you will find that you have names for some of your favorites.

And remember that a bird-feeder makes a fine Christmas present for a shut-in who may be able to spend many hours watching the birds.

NATURE TRAILS

BUILDING A NATURE TRAIL

A Nature Trail is a self-operating device for imparting information about some of the things found in nature, and located along a path. The information may be about rocks,
plants, animal signs, trees, insects at work, erosion, insect or animal homes, or anything else close to the path.

The path should be easy to follow and should lead to points
of interest. It should be well marked with labels, signs,
or guideposts that provide interesting information, and that
stimulate people to learn more.

The Nature Trail should be so laid out and labeled, that the
person following it needs no other guide. Labels and mark-
ers should tell where more information is available for the
item under consideration.

A Nature Trail need not be long. Often a few hundred feet
is sufficient. A tiny Nature Trail may be laid out inside a
terrarium.

Labels should be spaced so that one sign or label may be
seen from the previous one.

USES:

A Nature Trail affords one of the easiest ways to impart
    nature lore and to stimulate people to learn more.

MATERIALS:

A path through fields, woods, or marsh

Signs or labels such as the following

    Linen tags marked with India ink, waterproofed with
    spray-plastic, melted paraffin, or linseed oil.

    Masonite or plywood labels. Cover with two coats of
    flat white paint. Label with India ink and add two coats
    of varnish or plastic spray.

    Zinc sheets treated the same as the masonite or plywood.

File cards lettered with India ink and waterproofed in
the same manner as the linen tags.

HOW TO MAKE:

Vary the size and shape of the labels for interest.   Use
    imagination in designing the shapes and the lettering.
    One sign might use the shape of a leaf.   Another may
    include a picture or illustration cut from a magazine
    or pamphlet, cemented to a sign and waterproofed with
    shellac, varnish, or spray-plastic.

At the beginning of the trail place the first sign telling of the
    Nature Trail and its purpose.

Two of many ways suggested for stimulating interest along a Nature Trail. An exhibit, close to a Nature Trail, calls attention to many interesting things. Reference works near the end of the trail provide additional information to those whose curiosity has been aroused by the exhibit.

RECIPES FOR CRAFT PROJECTS

TERRAIN MODELING

Making models of camp sites; of home grounds; model rail-
roads; and other exhibits that feature fields, hills, and
streams, requires material to make the terrain stand out
in relief.

Here Are Five Formulas for Making Terrain Models:

1. 1 pint ordinary sawdust

    1 pint Plaster of Paris

    1/4 pint library paste

    Add just enough water to the paste to make it thin and runny. Stir in the plaster, then the sawdust, and knead to a doughy consistency. This formula hardens in 10 - 20 minutes.

2. 2 pints wet newspaper pulp

    1 pint Plaster of Paris

    1/4 teaspoon LePages Glue

    1/2 pint water

    Make paper pulp by rubbing wet newspapers between palms of the hands until ground to a pulp. Add the glue to the water. Stir in the plaster then the paper pulp. Knead to a doughy consistency. This formula takes about 3 hours to harden.

3. 1/2 pint wet newspaper pulp

    1/2 pint sifted, powdered dry clay

    1 teaspoon LePages Glue

    1 cup water

    Dissolve glue in water and add dry clay. Stir well and add wet paper pulp. Knead to a doughy consistency. This formula takes about 12 hours to harden.

4. 2 pints wet newspaper pulp

    2 pints of Plaster of Paris

    1/4 teaspoon Lepages Glue

    1/2 pint water

    Add glue to water. Stir in plaster, then paper pulp. Knead to a doughy consistency. Takes about 30 minutes to harden.

5. 1 pint sawdust

3/4 pint Plaster of Paris

1/2 pint library paste

3 drops LePages Glue

Dissolve paste in water to thin; add glue; stir in plaster then sawdust. Knead to a heavy doughy consistency. Takes about 8 hours to harden.

MODELING CLAY

1 cup flour

1/2 cup salt

1 teaspoon alum

Mix with enough water to make a very thick paste (lukewarm water is best). Wrap molding clay in wet cloths to keep it damp and pliable. Food colors may be used to color the clay. It can be kept indefinitely in a covered jar.

SALT AND FLOUR CLAY

Mix 1 cup salt

1/2 cup flour

1 cup water

Heat this mixture over a very low flame, stirring constantly until it is thick and rubbery. Knead when cooled. If too sticky, add more flour and knead well. Color with food coloring if desired. Use this clay for relief modeling, for figure modeling, bead making, etc.

NATIVE CLAYS FOR MODELING

Use clean, powdered, and sifted clay.

For each pound of native clay, mix in 1 tablespoon of dextrin (from a science equipment house), or Dexin (baby food) to help the clay to harden. Mix well, then add enough water to make a thick modeling clay.

Keep clay covered with wet cloths until used.

PAPIER—MÂCHE´

1/2 pound regular wall plaster

1/2 pound ground asbestos

Mix with water to a putty-like consistency

STARCH — SALT — PAPER BEADS

1 heaping tablespoon corn-
    starch

1 cup water

1/4 cup salt

1 cup shredded newspaper

Dissolve cornstarch in small amount of water. Bring cup of water to boil and add salt and cornstarch. Boil until clear. Add shredded newspaper and stir well. When cool, mold in bead shapes. Make hole for thread with needle or pin. Let dry and string. This material may be colored by adding food coloring.

FLOUR PASTE

1 pint flour

1 tablespoon powdered alum

1 cup boiling water

1 teaspoon oil of cloves

1 pint cold water.

Add alum to one cup boiling water. Mix flour and cold water and add gradually to boiling water containing a alum. Stir and cook until bluish color is evident. Remove from heat, add oil of cloves and stir well. Keep this paste in air-tight jars. It may be thinned by the addition of water.

FINGER PAINTS

1 1/2 cups laundry starch

1 quart boiling water

1 1/2 cups soap flakes

1/2 cup talcum powder

1/2 tablespoon powdered
     tempera paints

Mix starch and cold water to form thin paste. Add boiling water and cook until transparent, stirring constantly. Add talcum and stir. Add soap-flakes stirring well.

Glazed white papers such as shelf papers are excellent for finger-painting.

MORE FINGER PAINTS

3 tablespoons sugar

1/2 cup cornstarch

2 cups cold water

Mix all ingredients together and cook over low heat until well blended, stirring constantly. Food coloring may be added as desired.

To use, drop a small amount of paint on a sheet of moistened white paper. Make designs with the fingers, fork, knife, comb, brush, or other materials.

Finger paints are most useful for children's creative painting.

118

SELECTED BIBLIOGRAPHY

The following list of books, to the best knowledge of the a
author, provides the most useful references available for
the type of material included in this book.

"Campcraft, A Manual For Leaders Responsible For The
Organization Of Campcraft In The Summer Camp" by
Barbara Ellen Joy; Burgess Publishing Co., 426 South
Sixth St., Minneapolis 15, Minnesota; 1955 $2.75

"How To Make A Nature Museum" by Vinson Brown; Little
Brown and Co., Boston, Mass.; 1955 $2.50

"Nature Games And Activities" by Cassell; Harper and
Brothers, 49 E. 33rd St., New York 16, N. Y.; 1956
$2.50

"Creative Crafts For Campers" by Catherine T. Hammett
and Carol M. Horrocks; Association Press, 291 Broadway, New York 7, N. Y.; 1957 $6.95

"Campcraft A B C's" by Catherine T. Hammett; Girl Scouts
of the U.S.A., 155 E. 44th St., New York 17, N. Y.
1941 $1.25

"Your Own Book of Campcraft" by Catherine T. Hammett;
Pocket Books, Inc., 488 Madison Ave., New York;
1950 $.35

"Field Book Of Nature Activities" by William Hillcourt;
G. P. Putnam's Sons, 210 Madison Ave., New York 16,
N. Y.; 1950 $3.95

"Whittling Book" by Ben Hunt; Bruce Publishing Co.,
400 N. Broadway, Milwaukee 1, Wisconsin; 1944 $3.50

"Nature Crafts" by Ellsworth Jaeger; The Macmillan Co.,
60 Fifth Ave., New York 11, N. Y.; 1950 $2.50

"Easy Crafts" by Ellsworth Jaeger; The Macmillan Co.,
60 Fifth Ave., New York 11, N. Y.;

"Wildwood Wisdom" by Ellsworth Jaeger; The Macmillan Co.
60 Fifth Ave., New York 11, N. Y.;

"Woodcraft" by Bernard S. Mason; A. S. Barnes and Co.,
232 Madison Ave., New York 16, N. Y.; 1939 $2.75

"Nature Activities" by J. A. Partridge and D. E. Farwell;
Canadian Nature Magazine, 177 Jarvis St., Toronto;
1953 $.50

"Book Of Nature Hobbies" by Ted Pettit; Didier Publishers,
   660 Madison Ave. , New York; 1947 $3.50

"The Birch Bark Roll Of Woodcraft" by Ernest Thompson
   Seton; A. S. Barnes and Co. , New York; (Out of print)

"Things To Do With A Pocket Knife" by E. J. Tangerman;
   Remington Arms Co. , Inc. , Cutler Division, Bridgeport,
   Conn. ; 1934 Free

"Whittling And Woodcarving" by E. J. Tangerman;
   Whittlesey House, McGraw-Hill Book Co. , 330 West
   42nd St. , New York 36, N. Y. ; 1936 $6.00

"Conservation And Nature Activities" Audubon Society of
   Canada, 177 Jarvis St. , Toronto; 1951 $3.70

"Nature Activities For Summer Camps" National Audubon
   Society, 1000 Fifth St. , New York; 1950

"Whittling Is Easy With X-Acto" X-acto, Inc. , Long Island
   City 1, New York 1953 $.25

"Homespun Crafts" by Kenneth Baillie; Bruce Publishing Co. ,
   400 North Broadway, Milwaukee 1, Wisconsin; 1952
   $3.00

"Arts and Crafts - A Practical Handbook" by Marguerite Ickis;
   A. S. Barnes and Co. , 232 Madison Ave. , New York 16,
   N. Y. ; 1943 $4.00

"The Book Of Arts And Crafts" by Marguerite Ickis and
   Reba S. Ash; Association Press, 291 Broadway,
   New York 7, N. Y. ; 1954 $4.95

"The Art Of Driftwood And Dried Arrangements" by Tatsuo
   Ishimoto; Crown Publishers Inc. , 419 4th Ave. ,
   New York; 1951 $2.95

"Nature Recreation" by William G. Vinal; McGraw-Hill Book
   Co. , 330 West 42nd St. , New York 36, N. Y. ; 1940
   $3.25

"Arts And Crafts With Inexpensive Materials" Girl Scouts
   of the U.S.A. , 155 East 44th St. , New York 17, N. Y. ;
   1947 $.50

"Craft Projects For Camp And Playground" National Recreation Association, 8 West 8th St. , New York 11, N. Y.
   1953 $.50

"Nature Crafts For Camp And Playground" National Recreation, 8 West 8th St. , New York 11, N. Y.

"Keeping Idle Hands Busy" by Marion R. Spear; Burgess
     Publishing Co., 426 South Sixth St., Minneapolis 15,
     Minn.; 1958 $2.25

"How To Do Wood Carving" by John L. Lacey; Fawcett
     Book 248, Fawcett Publications, Inc., Greenwich,
     Conn.; $.75

"Use Of Native Craft Materials" by Margaret E. Shanklin;
     The Manual Arts Press, Peoria, Illinois; 1947

"Creative Handicrafts" by M. R. Hutchins; Sentinel Books,
     112 East Nineteenth St., New York; 1938

"Folk Arts And Crafts" by Marguerite Ickis; Association
     Press, 291 Broadway, New York 7, N. Y.; 1958 $5.95

"4-H Club Insect Manual" Misc. Publication No. 318,
     U. S. Department of Agriculture, Washington, D. C.;
     1939; (Also available through your local Extension
     Service Offices)